MARIE ASSELIN

FRENCH APPETIZERS

PHOTOGRAPHS BY
CATHERINE CÔTÉ

GIBBS SMITH
TO ENRICH AND INSPIRE HUMANKIND

To my closest friends,
with whom I'll gladly share *l'apéro* any night of the week.
You know who you are.

First Edition
23 22 21 20 19   5 4 3 2 1

Text © 2019 Marie Asselin
Photographs © 2019 Catherine Côté

Published by
Gibbs Smith
P.O. Box 667
Layton, Utah 84041

1.800.835.4993 orders
www.gibbs-smith.com

Designed by Mina Bach
Printed and bound in Hong Kong
Gibbs Smith books are printed on either recycled, 100% post-consumer waste, FSC-certified papers or on paper
produced from sustainable PEFC-certified forest/controlled wood source. Learn more at www.pefc.org.

Library of Congress Cataloging-in-Publication Data

Names: Asselin, Marie, author.
Title: French appetizers / Marie Asselin ; Photographs by Catherine Côté.
Description: First edition. | Layton, Utah : Gibbs Smith, [2019]
Identifiers: LCCN 2018032229 | ISBN 9781423651024 (hardcover)
Subjects: LCSH: Appetizers. | Cooking, French. | LCGFT: Cookbooks.
Classification: LCC TX740 .A87 2019 | DDC 641.81/20944--dc23
LC record available at https://lccn.loc.gov/2018032229

CONTENTS

ACKNOWLEDGMENTS

I'm grateful to Michelle Branson, senior editor and head of the cookbook team at Gibbs Smith, for trusting me with a second cookbook project. I loved working on this delicious book, and I hope our collaboration will continue to blossom.

Thank you to my recipe testers for putting up with the overwhelmed recipe developer I was during the creation of this book, and for being so extremely helpful with making the recipes as close to perfection as they can possibly be: Isabelle, Marie-Andrée, Fanny, Gabrielle, Rachel, Liliana, Lisa, Kim, Samantha, Kate, Suzanne, Paula, Leigh, Lucia, and Sara. Special thanks to my pro recipe tester, Janice Lawandi, for sprinkling your scientific knowledge into my baked goods.

Thank you to my friend and close collaborator, food photographer Catherine Côté, for bringing my recipes to life.

Thank you to my parents, Réjeane and Jean-Luc, for being my biggest supporters and for instilling the love of food and get-togethers in me from a very young age.

Thank you to my close friends, with whom I've shared so many *apéros* already. There are countless more to come!

And finally, thank you to my partner, Eric, and to my son, Jules, for adding light to my every day. Thank you for being such loving supporters, willing tasters, and gracious critics.

INTRODUCTION

L'apéro: How the French do cocktail hour

"Vous venez pour l'apéro?"

My friends and I exchange this question every week. Calling (or more often now, texting) a friend to ask, "Will you come visit for l'apéro?" is a way to invite them over to have a drink and some bites before dinner. Often, l'apéro lasts only a couple of hours, usually from five to seven, but sometimes it'll last all through the night, evolving into a casual dinner.

"L'apéro" is short for *l'apéritif,* which is the name of a drink served in the early evening to whet your appetite. In French cities, people have l'apéro in restaurants and bars, with servers bringing salty snacks to go with your drinks, but this tradition of getting together after work to relax with a drink before dinner is also a full-blown ritual that is often hosted at home, accompanied by a variety of bites or appetizers that can be generous enough to become dinner itself.

L'apéro is in my blood: all through my childhood, I watched my parents host it. Even when my mother hosted a sit-down dinner, she'd always first gather guests in the living room for l'apéro. She'd ask my dad to help with the drinks while she served crackers and pâtés she'd saved specifically for such occasions. When I was a young adult, l'apéro was pretty much code for "house party." I'd get a bunch of friends over and we'd drink and nibble our way through the night against a background of very loud music. When I lived in Paris for a while in 2009, I could enjoy l'apéro the Parisian way. I'd watch friends effortlessly unfold an array of delicious treats they'd gathered at their favorite gourmet stores on the way home from work. Such evenings would invariably stretch far into the night—and sometimes until the wee hours of the morning.

Now that I'm a parent, l'apéro is how I keep connected with friends who have families, too. All parents know having sit-down meals and meaningful conversations can be challenges when kids are around. L'apéro relieves you of that stress. Because it's served early, kids can get together and play their little hearts out while we, the adults, enjoy a glass of wine and some delicious food. My trick is to serve a "mini apéro" to kids on a play table—veggies, cheese, cured meats, and bread—so they can keep busy and eat dinner at their own pace, while adults can (finally) take an hour or two to catch up. That way, everyone goes back home in time for bedtime, with bellies and hearts full.

L'apéro is a casual affair. If I invite friends over for l'apéro, they won't expect me to dress the table or even clean up the house. On the simplest nights, we'll huddle in the kitchen, share salty snacks, and wash it all down with cold beer or wine. On planned-ahead nights, I'll expand the selection to include a few homemade bites. On celebratory nights, I'll plan a whole menu that features several appetizers to create a full meal called an *"apéro*

dînatoire," and sometimes go the extra mile to pair each plate with an appropriate wine.

I believe l'apéro is the best way to host friends and family, and my goal is to convince you of its merits. I filled this book with tips to get you started, menu ideas from the simplest to the most elegant, lots of French-inspired appetizer recipes to help you assemble inspiring meals, and even versatile syrups you can keep at the back of the fridge to shake and stir impressive drinks in the nick of time. Whatever time you have on your hands, whatever the occasion you want to celebrate, I hope you'll have friends over for l'apéro. *Santé!*

For more recipes and day-to-day inspiration, visit my blog FoodNouveau.com **and follow me on Instagram** @foodnouveau. **Share the recipes you make from the book at** #FrenchAppetizers.

About the recipes in this book

The recipes in this book were inspired by my French-Canadian heritage, the love my parents and my extended family have for everything French, and my frequent travels to France. In the recipes, I use quintessential French ingredients, but also more exotic ones that have become daily staples in France and around the world. Following the same line of thought, I created recipes inspired by classic French dishes, as well as ones influenced by the modern food I see and taste when I travel to Paris. The cuisine of a people is an ever-evolving one after all.

What to serve for l'apéro

A classic apéro features charcuteries, pâtés, or rillettes served with a sliced baguette and additional nibbles such as cornichons and olives. Modern French apéros often include chips, nuts, and even popcorn because they're so convenient and even—dare I say—trendy. Who doesn't like salty snacks with a drink? I like to combine both approaches: I'll start with a combination of store-bought items, such as sausages, olives, and some fancy chips, and add some crudités for good balance. Depending on the occasion, and if time allows, I'll prepare homemade dips and more elaborate bites.

Whatever food you serve, make sure it can easily be eaten in one or two bites. Your guests will likely be standing with a glass in one hand, so you need to make things easy for them. Cut or slice food into bite-size pieces and keep napkins on hand at all times. The appetizers included in this book should usually be served family-style—that is, placed on a side table, kitchen island, or dining table, along with small plates and utensils, so everyone can help themselves.

Drinks served for l'apéro are usually lighter in alcohol levels—the night is just getting started, after all. You'll never go wrong by chilling a bottle or two of sparkling, white, or rosé wine. To stir things up, keep one or two of the syrups included in the Drinks chapter (page 117) at the back of the fridge, and you'll always be a few steps away from exciting virgin drinks, sparkling kirs, and easy cocktails. Make sure to keep water (still and sparkling) and extra glasses on hand.

How to plan a stress-free apéro

L'apéro is meant to be a relaxing hiatus in your busy day, so hosting it at home shouldn't be a source of stress. You should be able to lay out the food and enjoy the moment, just as your guests do—not spend the whole evening in the kitchen. Here are my top tips to help you host a stress-free apéro:

- **Keep staples on hand for last-minute entertaining.** I always keep a bottle of white wine and a jar of olives in the fridge (my Orange and Fennel Marinated Olives on page 31 keep refrigerated for weeks), plus some crackers and a jar or two of shelf-stable terrines and rillettes in the pantry. With such basic items on hand, you'll always be ready for spontaneous gatherings.

- **Use your freezer.** Keep a sheet of puff pastry in the freezer, and you'll always be only minutes away from impressive Palmiers (page 51). When you have time on your hands, make a few batches of Shortcrust Pastry (page 26) and freeze them, so you can quickly whip up a Cherry Tomato, Spinach, and Goat Cheese Sheet Pan Quiche (page 60), a Pear and Blue Cheese Savory Galette (page 62), or some Chamomile Lemon Tartlets (page 99) later on. Many more of the recipes in this book freeze well, such as the Goat Cheese Truffles (page 32), Gougères, Four Ways (page 38), savory cakes, and meatballs. Keep them on hand and you'll always be ready to upgrade your apéro game.

- **Prep ahead.** If you're planning a more ambitious apéro, or even a whole small-plate meal, pick a combination of recipes that will allow you to do most of the prep ahead of time. The only things you should be doing once your guests arrive are some last-minute baking or reheating (of things you kept in the freezer), garnishing, and serving. See page 10 for prep-ahead menu ideas.

- **Ask for help.** L'apéro is, at its very core, a friendly, casual event. Your guests may spend the whole evening chatting in the kitchen, so why not ask them to help you prep and serve the food? I also like to host apéro potluck nights, for which I ask every friend or family to bring one dish to share. We then put all the food on the table and enjoy our time together. It's always fun to discover what everyone chooses to bring! Don't forget to recruit a few friends to help with clean up: it will get done quickly while you keep chatting—and drinking wine.

Looking for inspiration? Check out my menu ideas on page 10 to get started.
Set the mood! Listen to French-inspired cocktail hour music: http://bit.ly/FrenchAppetizersPlaylist

Menu Ideas

These menus are meant to get your creative juices flowing. Feel free to substitute dishes or to prepare only one or two dishes from scratch, filling up the menu with nuts, crudités, and cured meats. Desserts are always optional, but leave your guests on a sweet note.

The Quick and Easy

Feeling lazy? I don't blame you. This is the kind of apéro I host most weeks. Keep sheets of puff pastry in the freezer, jars of pesto or tapenade in the fridge, and cans of quality fish in the pantry, and you'll get this menu done in no time.

- Palmiers, Three Ways (page 51—use store-bought pesto or tapenade if you don't have time to make your own)
- Instant Fish Rillettes, Three Ways (page 34)
- Crackers (homemade, see page 42, or store-bought)
- Selection of cured meats and charcuteries
- Quality store-bought dark chocolate

The Luxurious

This menu is for those celebratory nights such as birthday parties, wedding anniversaries, or New Year's Eve. The recipes are meant to impress, but you can still do most of the prep ahead of time, leaving you free to enjoy the event, too.

- Gougères, Four Ways (page 38)
- Cauliflower and Apple Velouté (page 86)—with crab or lobster topping
- Beef Tartare and Marinated Mushroom Verrine (page 90)
- Pear and Blue Cheese Savory Galette (page 62)—make the shortcrust pastry days ahead of time, and bake the galette a few hours before your guests arrive
- Spiced Madeleines with Salted Caramel Sauce (page 93)

The Pack Up and Go

Moving l'apéro to the park? Bringing l'apéro to a friend who can't cook? These prep-ahead, highly portable, no-heat-required recipes will add a festive tone anywhere you go.

- Cherry Tomato, Strawberry, and Basil Gazpacho (page 84)
- Beet, Goat Cheese, and Orange Dip (page 25) served with crackers or pita chips
- Caramelized Fennel, Lemon, and Comté Cake (page 55) or Zucchini, Cured Ham, and Goat Cheese Muffins (page 58)
- Chocolate and Tahini Sablés (page 105)

The Vegan

Hosting vegan friends? No need to prepare separate dishes just for them! Here's a delightful vegan menu all your guests will enjoy.

- Cherry Tomato, Strawberry, and Basil Gazpacho (page 84)
- Fig, Walnut, and Orange Fougasse (page 68)
- Carrot, Pistachio, and Hummus Verrine (page 88) or Pistachio Falafel (page 44) served with Any-Bean Hummus (page 18, or store-bought)
- Triple Lemon Dark Chocolate Truffles (page 112)—use vegan chocolate and substitute soy or coconut cream for the heavy cream

The Feeding a Crowd

Is your cocktail hour turning into a house party? These make-ahead recipes will allow you to feed lots of hungry people in a blink.

- Orange and Fennel Marinated Olives (page 31)
- Marinated Mushrooms (page 41) and Goat Cheese Truffles, Four Ways (page 32) served with fresh or toasted baguette slices (see page 74)
- Cherry Tomato, Spinach, and Goat Cheese Sheet Pan Quiche (page 60)
- Strawberry-Lemon Yogurt Sheet Cake (page 108)

The Dairy Free

French-inspired recipes can be generous in butter, cheese, and other dairy products. If you're looking to cut down on such products, or want to prepare a lighter apéro, here's the menu for you.

- Green Olive and Za'atar Tapenade (page 14) served with Crunchy Seed Crackers (page 42) or pita chips
- Fresh Herb Pissaladière (page 71)
- Chicken and Olive Meatballs (page 47) served with Classic Pistou (page 13)—make sure to omit the Parmesan
- Berry Cups with Green Tea and Honey Syrup (page 111)

BASICS AND CONDIMENTS

Bases et condiments

CLASSIC PISTOU

Makes about 1 cup

Ever wondered about the difference between French pistou and Italian pesto? It's simple: pistou does not contain pine nuts, and the cheese is optional, too. There probably are as many pistou recipes as there are French cooks, but I like mine like Julia Child made hers—with a bit of tomato flesh blended in, which adds a nice touch of acidity. When you store it in a jar, pour a thin layer of olive oil to fully cover the top of the pistou before closing the jar. This will keep the pistou from browning. Serve with crudités or Chicken and Olive Meatballs (page 47), as a topping for soup or a spread over baguette slices, or in a sandwich. Pistou can also dress up pasta or serve as a condiment for grilled or braised meats, fish, and seafood.

   1 clove garlic
   1 teaspoon kosher salt
   2 ounces fresh basil leaves (about 2 cups, gently packed)
   ¼ cup chopped plum tomato
   ¼ cup extra virgin olive oil
   ¼ cup grated Parmesan cheese (optional)

Add all the ingredients to a food processor. Process until finely and evenly chopped, scraping down the sides if needed. Process longer for a smoother texture. Store in an airtight jar in the refrigerator for up to 1 week.

*See page 17 for photo.

TAPENADE, THREE WAYS

Each variation makes about 1 cup

I always keep one or two jars of tapenade at the back of my fridge. It's a versatile condiment that can be served with crudités, crackers, pita chips, fresh or toasted baguette slices (see page 74), grilled or braised meats, fish, and seafood. It can also dress up pasta. Tapenade pretty much keeps forever if refrigerated in an airtight jar, and it couldn't be easier to make: simply blend everything together and enjoy.

Black Olive and Lemon Tapenade

1 cup oil-packed pitted black olives (such as Kalamata), drained (about 5 ounces)

2 tablespoons extra virgin olive oil

1 tablespoon drained capers

2 anchovy fillets

1 tablespoon finely grated lemon zest (about 1 lemon)

2 tablespoons freshly squeezed lemon juice (about ½ lemon)

1 tablespoon chopped fresh flat-leaf parsley

½ clove garlic, chopped (about ½ teaspoon)

Green Olive and Za'atar Tapenade

1 cup firmly packed pitted green olives (such as Castelvetrano or Cerignola), drained

2 tablespoons extra virgin olive oil

2 tablespoons toasted sesame seeds

2 anchovy fillets

1 tablespoon chopped preserved lemon rind

1 teaspoon za'atar

1 teaspoon fresh thyme leaves (optional)

½ clove garlic, chopped (about ½ teaspoon)

Sun-Dried Tomato and Basil Tapenade

¾ cup drained oil-packed sun-dried tomatoes

¼ cup extra virgin olive oil

¼ cup firmly packed fresh basil leaves, chopped

2 tablespoons toasted whole almonds

2 tablespoons grated Parmesan cheese

1 tablespoon freshly squeezed lemon juice

1 tablespoon drained capers

½ clove garlic, chopped (about ½ teaspoon)

½ teaspoon kosher salt

Add all the ingredients to a food processor or use a hand blender. Process or blend until finely and evenly chopped, scraping down the sides if needed. The tapenade will be quite thick and chunky. For a smoother, creamier texture, add an additional 2 tablespoons olive oil and process until desired consistency.

MAYO, THREE WAYS

Each variation makes about 1 cup

Making mayo from scratch for the first time can be revelatory: it's light and creamy and completely different from the store-bought stuff. The taste of homemade mayo highly depends on the quality and freshness of the oil you use to make it, so make sure to use the best quality you can afford.

½ cup smooth-tasting oil (such as vegetable, sunflower, or grapeseed)
¼ cup extra virgin olive oil
1 egg
2 tablespoons freshly squeezed lemon juice (about ½ lemon)
1 teaspoon Dijon mustard
½ teaspoon kosher salt

Classic Mayo

Combine the oils in a single measuring cup.

Combine the egg, lemon juice, mustard, and salt in a blender. With it running on the lowest speed, add the oil in a thin stream. The mayo will come together in seconds. Scrape down the sides if needed. For thicker mayo, add up to an additional ¼ cup oil. Taste and adjust seasoning or add more lemon juice if needed. Store in an airtight jar in the refrigerator for up to 1 week.

Fresh Herb Mayo

After the mayo is emulsified, add 2 to 4 tablespoons finely chopped mixed herbs (use any combination of parsley, chives, basil, oregano, or dill). Pulse to combine. Refrigerate in an airtight jar for at least 1 hour to allow the flavors to develop. Fresh Herb Mayo will keep for up to 1 week in the refrigerator.

Aïoli (Garlic Mayo)

Add 1 grated or puréed plump clove garlic (about 1 tablespoon) along with the egg, lemon juice, mustard, and salt. Proceed with the main recipe. Refrigerate in an airtight jar for at least 1 hour to allow the flavors to develop. Aïoli will keep for up to 1 week in the refrigerator.

Clockwise from top left: Classic Pistou (page 13), Classic Mayo, Anchoïade (Anchovy Dip) (page 24).

ANY-BEAN HUMMUS

Makes about 2 cups

Hummus isn't French, but it has become such an apéro staple in France and around the world in recent years that I couldn't help but include it in this book. What's handy about this recipe is that you can use *any* canned beans you have on hand for an amazingly creamy, flavorful, delicious result—every time. Believe me, I tried them all! Hummus is a great make-ahead recipe, but it's also quick enough to whip up last minute. Serve with Crunchy Seed Crackers (page 42), pita chips, crudités, or Pistachio Falafel Bites (page 44), or use as a spread on toasted baguette slices (see page 74), or in a sandwich.

1 (15.5-ounce) can chickpeas, white beans (such as cannellini), lentils, soy beans, kidney beans, black beans, or mixed beans, rinsed and drained

1 tablespoon finely grated lemon zest (about 1 lemon)

¼ cup freshly squeezed lemon juice (about 1 lemon)

2 tablespoons extra virgin olive oil

2 tablespoons tahini

1 clove garlic, chopped

1 teaspoon za'atar

½ teaspoon kosher salt

Freshly ground black pepper, to taste

To serve

Extra virgin olive oil

French Everything Flavoring Mix (page 28), or toasted sesame seeds

Sea salt flakes

Crushed black pepper

Add all the hummus ingredients to a food processor. Process until smooth. Depending on the beans you're using, you may need to add water to reach a creamy consistency. Add water, 1 tablespoon at a time, processing thoroughly and checking the texture before adding more. Taste and adjust the seasoning if needed. Store in an airtight container in the refrigerator for up to 1 week.

To serve, transfer the hummus to a shallow plate and create a nice swirl using the back of a spoon. Generously drizzle with additional olive oil, and then sprinkle with French Everything Flavoring Mix, sea salt flakes, and crushed black pepper.

EGGPLANT CAVIAR

Makes about 1 cup

Caviar d'aubergine, or eggplant caviar, is another cocktail hour staple in France. With origins in the Mediterranean and the Middle East, this creamy and slightly zesty purée of roasted eggplant is a delicious dip, but it's also an excellent sandwich or wrap spread. My favorite way to use it is in Baked Croque Monsieur Fingers (page 78), but you can serve it with crudités or pita chips or over toasted baguette slices (see page 74).

1 large eggplant (about 1 pound)

2 teaspoons extra virgin olive oil

4 cloves garlic, unpeeled

2 shallots, halved

2 tablespoons chopped mixed fresh herbs (a combination of mint, parsley, and basil)

1 tablespoon extra virgin olive oil

2 tablespoons freshly squeezed lemon juice (about ½ lemon)

1 teaspoon kosher salt

¼ teaspoon crushed red pepper or freshly ground black pepper

Preheat oven to 425°F. Line a baking sheet with aluminum foil. Halve the eggplant lengthwise then transfer to the prepared baking sheet, cut side up. Using a sharp, pointy knife, prick the flesh all over. Drizzle each eggplant half with 1 teaspoon of the olive oil, quickly rubbing it over the flesh (the oil will absorb quickly). Top the eggplant with the garlic and shallots. Roast for 40 minutes, or until the flesh is very soft. Remove from the oven and loosely wrap the aluminum foil over the eggplant to create a "steam room." Let rest for 15 minutes.

Transfer the shallots to a food processor. Squeeze the garlic flesh out of the skins and into the food processor. Scoop out the eggplant flesh into the food processor, discarding the skins. Add the herbs, olive oil, lemon juice, salt, and red pepper. Process until smooth, scraping down the sides a couple of times along the way. Store in an airtight container in the refrigerator for up to 1 week.

Clockwise from top right: Roasted Red Pepper and Hazelnut Dip, Crunchy Seed Crackers (page 42), Beet, Goat Cheese, and Orange Dip (page 25).

ROASTED RED PEPPER AND HAZELNUT DIP

Makes about 1 cup

This bright-red, dairy-free dip is thickened with toasted hazelnuts, which also add a delightful nutty flavor to the condiment. You can buy toasted and peeled hazelnuts, but they're cheaper and they keep longer if you buy them raw. Serve with Crunchy Seed Crackers (page 42), meatballs, crudités, or pita chips, spread over toasted baguette slices (see page 74), or in sandwiches.

¾ cup drained, coarsely chopped roasted red peppers

¼ cup toasted hazelnuts, coarsely chopped (see page 104)

1 tablespoon extra virgin olive oil

8 large fresh basil leaves, chopped

1 clove garlic

½ teaspoon kosher salt

Pinch of crushed red pepper

Add all the ingredients to a food processor or use a hand blender. Process or blend until smooth. Store in an airtight container in the refrigerator for up to 1 week.

ANCHOÏADE (ANCHOVY DIP)

Makes about ½ cup

Anchovies can be an acquired taste. They're irresistibly salty and intensely flavorful, which means the smallest quantity can lift the flavor of a dish in a blink. Anchoïade is a loose sauce that the French traditionally use as a dip for crudités. I also like to use it to dress pasta and spread over Fresh Herb Pissaladière (page 71) or toasted baguette slices (see page 74).

3.5 ounces oil-packed anchovy fillets, drained
3 tablespoons extra virgin olive oil
1 tablespoon red wine vinegar
1 teaspoon capers
1 clove garlic
Freshly ground black pepper, to taste

In a food processor, or using a hand blender, combine all the ingredients. Pulse until the texture resembles a coarse pesto. Add more oil if needed. Alternatively, you can finely chop the ingredients and combine them with a mortar and pestle. Store in an airtight jar in the refrigerator for up to 2 weeks.

*See page 17 for photo.

BEET, GOAT CHEESE, AND ORANGE DIP

Makes about 1¼ cups

Here's another spectacular treat to add to your apéro lineup. This sweet, creamy dip with a deep fuchsia color will gladly welcome any dipping vehicle, but it's so good you'll probably want to eat it by the spoonful. You can roast your own beets or buy increasingly available fresh roasted and peeled beets, which you'll find vacuum-packed in the produce section of the grocery store. Serve with Crunchy Seed Crackers (page 42), crudités, or pita chips, spread over toasted baguette slices (see page 74), or in sandwiches.

3 medium beets, roasted and peeled

4 ounces log-style goat cheese

1 tablespoon finely grated orange zest (about ½ orange)

2 tablespoons freshly squeezed orange juice (about ½ orange)

1 tablespoon rice wine vinegar or white balsamic vinegar

1 teaspoon honey

1 small clove garlic

½ teaspoon ground coriander

½ teaspoon kosher salt

Add all the ingredients to a food processor or use a hand blender. Process until smooth. Store in an airtight container in the refrigerator for up to 1 week.

*See page 22 for photo.

SHORTCRUST PASTRY

Makes 1 crust (enough for 1 large tart, 1 galette, or 18 mini tarts)

I used to shy away from making my own pie crusts because I found all the recipes I tried so difficult to work with. This shortcrust pastry recipe changed everything. It's buttery, super flaky, and versatile: you can make it whole wheat or even sweet for desserts. The fact that I also now roll out the dough before I refrigerate it for resting—a tip I picked up from Parisian cookbook writer Clotilde Dusoulier—was also a game changer. When you roll it fresh, the dough is supple and spreads like a charm, without cracking. Double the recipe to make a Cherry Tomato, Spinach, and Goat Cheese Sheet Pan Quiche (page 60).

½ cup (4 ounces) unsalted butter, chilled

1½ cups all-purpose flour

¼ teaspoon kosher salt

1 egg

2 tablespoons ice water

Cut the butter into small cubes and place on a small plate. Freeze for 20 minutes.

Food processor method Pulse the flour and salt together. Add the butter and process for 10 continuous seconds, until the mixture looks like coarse breadcrumbs. Add the egg and process for 5 seconds. Add the ice water and process for 20 seconds. The dough should now start clumping together. Turn the mixture out onto a work surface. The mixture will still be grainy but should hold together when pressed. Using your hands, gather the dough into a ball then flatten into a disk, kneading it as lightly as possible.

Hand method In a large mixing bowl, whisk the flour and salt together. Add the butter and the egg, cutting into the flour using a pastry cutter or your hands until the mixture has a pea-like consistency. Drizzle in the water and continue cutting just to combine. Gather the dough into a ball then flatten into a disk, kneading it as lightly as possible.

Roll out the dough as needed (see tip), or wrap the dough tightly in plastic wrap and refrigerate for up to 3 days. You can also freeze the dough for up to 1 month, wrapped in plastic wrap and placed in a freezer bag.

Tip: It's easier to roll out dough just after it has been mixed together, as opposed to rolling it after refrigeration. If you're making shortcrust pastry right before you need to use it, gather it into a disk, set it on a lightly floured surface, and roll it out to the required size. Transfer to a tart pan, a baking sheet if making a galette (see page 62), muffin pans if making tartlets, or a sheet pan if making a Cherry Tomato, Spinach, and Goat Cheese Sheet Pan Quiche (page 60). Refrigerate for 30 minutes to an hour. Use as instructed by the recipe.

VARIATIONS

- **Whole-wheat crust** Substitute one-third of the all-purpose flour for whole-wheat flour.

- **Sweet crust for desserts** Add 1 tablespoon granulated sugar to the flour mixture.

FRENCH EVERYTHING FLAVORING MIX

Makes about ½ cup

Inspired by the everything seasoning that's often used to flavor bagels, I created this French-infused version to add crunch and flavor to anything and everything. Serve liberally sprinkled over hummus and dips, Goat Cheese Truffles, Four Ways (page 32), Palmiers, Three Ways (page 51), or salads. Save time by making a double or triple batch; the flavoring mix will keep in an airtight jar in the pantry for weeks.

2 tablespoons toasted sesame seeds

2 tablespoons poppy seeds

2 tablespoons herbes de Provence*

1 tablespoon coarsely ground fennel seeds

1 tablespoon dried garlic flakes

1 tablespoon sea salt flakes (such as fleur de sel)

1 teaspoon coarsely ground black pepper

Combine all the ingredients in an airtight jar. Store at room temperature for up to 1 month.

*Herbes de Provence is a dried herb mix that typically combines savory, marjoram, thyme, rosemary, and oregano.

SMALL BITES

Grignotines

Orange and Fennel Marinated Olives

Goat Cheese Truffles, Four Ways

Instant Fish Rillettes, Three Ways

Warm Brown Butter Bourbon Radishes

Gougères, Four Ways

Marinated Mushrooms

Crunchy Seed Crackers

Pistachio Falafel

Chicken and Olive Meatballs

Savory Sablés, Three Ways

Palmiers, Three Ways

Left: Orange and Fennel Marinated Olives; right: Marinated Mushrooms (page 41).

ORANGE AND FENNEL MARINATED OLIVES

Makes about 2 cups

If you asked me to illustrate cocktail hour, I'd probably draw a bowl of olives. I usually double this recipe and store the olives in a large Mason jar at the back of my fridge, where they'll keep on soaking up flavor for weeks. Serve these warm and you're guaranteed to impress your guests.

1 medium orange

2 cups large green olives (such as Castelvetrano or Cerignola), drained

½ cup extra virgin olive oil

2 cloves garlic, crushed with the side of a knife

½ teaspoon fennel pollen*, or 1 teaspoon crushed fennel seeds

1 teaspoon crushed black pepper

1 bay leaf

Zest the orange in wide strips using a vegetable peeler. Juice the orange.

Combine all the ingredients in a medium saucepan. Warm over medium-low heat for about 5 minutes to release the flavors, closely watching the garlic and stirring as necessary so it doesn't brown. Transfer to an airtight jar and let the flavors infuse at room temperature for at least 1 hour. Always bring the olives back to room temperature before serving. Alternatively, serve them slightly reheated.

*Fennel pollen is a yellow and green coarse powder that is hand collected from wild fennel. Its flavor is different from fennel seed or anise: it has a mellower anise flavor yet adds a lot of punch to dishes—a little fennel pollen goes a long way. You'll find fennel pollen in specialty food stores or online.

GOAT CHEESE TRUFFLES, FOUR WAYS

Makes 20 truffles

Don't you think goat cheese truffles have a vintage charm? Yet they're so easy to make and so popular that I guarantee you they still deserve a spot on your apéro table. You can even make the truffles in advance and freeze them. They'll thaw at room temperature in 15 minutes. Roll them in the flavorings of your choice right before serving with fresh or toasted baguette slices (see page 74).

8 ounces log-style goat cheese, room temperature

1 tablespoon extra virgin olive oil

1 teaspoon crushed black pepper

Pinch of kosher salt

Fresh Herb Goat Cheese Truffles

½ cup mixed fresh herbs, finely chopped (such as basil, marjoram, oregano, parsley, rosemary, and dill)

1 tablespoon freshly grated lemon zest (about 1 lemon)

Orange-Walnut Goat Cheese Truffles

½ cup finely chopped walnuts

1 tablespoon freshly grated orange zest (about ½ orange)

¼ teaspoon ground cumin

Sesame-Coriander Goat Cheese Truffles

¼ cup toasted sesame seeds (white or black, or a combination)

¼ cup finely chopped cilantro

½ teaspoon ground coriander

French Everything Goat Cheese Truffles

¼ cup French Everything Flavoring Mix (page 28)

2 tablespoons finely chopped flat-leaf parsley

Place the cheese in a large mixing bowl. Using a fork, mash to soften then whisk to make smooth. Whisk in the olive oil, pepper, and salt.

In a small bowl, combine the ingredients for the flavor option you wish to make. Add the flavor ingredients to the cheese, and mix to combine. Use a cookie scoop to create truffles and arrange on a serving plate or in an airtight container. Alternatively, use two spoons to pick up portions of cheese mixture then gently roll into balls using your hands. Refrigerate for at least 30 minutes to let the flavors infuse, or up to 3 days.

INSTANT FISH RILLETTES, THREE WAYS

Makes about 1 cup

Rillettes are classic French spreads often made with shredded meat. While meat rillettes are a time-consuming project, fish rillettes come together in a flash. I call my recipe "instant" because all you have to do is open a can of fish, and mix in the flavorings. Serve with Crunchy Seed Crackers (page 42) or with fresh or toasted baguette slices (see page 74).

Salmon and Capers

1 (6-ounce) can salmon (preferably a wild pacific salmon variety)

2 tablespoons Classic Mayo (page 16)

1 tablespoon extra virgin olive oil

1 tablespoon freshly squeezed lemon juice

1 tablespoon capers, coarsely chopped

1 tablespoon chives

½ teaspoon sea salt flakes

Freshly ground black pepper, to taste

Tuna and Preserved Lemon

1 (6-ounce) can light tuna, drained

2 tablespoons plain yogurt, or Classic Mayo (page 16)

1 tablespoon extra virgin olive oil

1 tablespoon finely chopped preserved lemon rind

1 tablespoon finely chopped fresh mint

1 tablespoon finely chopped fresh flat-leaf parsley

¼ teaspoon ground cumin

½ teaspoon sea salt flakes

Freshly ground black pepper, to taste

Sardines and Olives

2 (3.75-ounce) cans olive oil-packed boneless, skinless sardines, drained

2 tablespoons plain yogurt, or mayo

2 tablespoons finely chopped green olives

1 tablespoon extra virgin olive oil

1 tablespoon freshly squeezed lemon juice

1 tablespoon finely chopped flat-leaf parsley

1 teaspoon wholegrain mustard or Dijon mustard

Pinch cayenne pepper

½ teaspoon sea salt flakes

Add the fish to a bowl and use a fork to flake it. Add the remaining ingredients and mix to thoroughly combine. Transfer to a glass jar. Refrigerate for up to 3 days.

WARM BROWN BUTTER BOURBON RADISHES

Serves 4 to 6

If you know someone who claims they don't like radishes, make this dish for them. I've converted many radish skeptics with it. Sautéing radishes mellows out their peppery edge, and the warm, nutty brown butter and bourbon dressing irresistibly coats their ever-so-slightly softened flesh. This dish is at its very best when made with the freshest summer radishes—you can even use them with the leaves on.

1 bunch fresh radishes (regular or French breakfast)

¼ cup (2 ounces) butter

1 tablespoon bourbon, whiskey, or water

2 tablespoons chopped fresh chives

Finely grated zest of ½ lemon

½ teaspoon fennel pollen or crushed fennel seeds

Freshly ground black pepper, to taste

Sea salt flakes, to taste

Trim and thoroughly clean the radishes. Halve or quarter if they're large; you want bite-size pieces of radish.

In a skillet over medium heat, melt the butter. Swirling the pan from time to time, cook the butter until it browns and lets off a delightful nutty aroma. Mix in the bourbon, simmer for 30 seconds, and then toss in the radishes. Cook over high heat for 3 minutes, tossing radishes regularly to coat with butter. Stir in the chives then transfer to a serving plate. Sprinkle with zest, fennel, pepper, and salt. Serve immediately.

GOUGÈRES, FOUR WAYS

Makes 36 gougères

Gougères have been my signature apéro treat for years. They're so festive and delicious I call them my instant mood lifters. Plus, Gougères can be made several hours ahead. If you've never made *pâte à choux* before, fear not: it's much easier to whip up than you probably think. See them made in my online video class: http://bit.ly/chouxvideoclass. Baking your first batch of Gougères will give you confidence, and I'll bet that before long, they'll become your signature treat too.

1 cup water

3 tablespoons unsalted butter, diced

¾ teaspoon kosher salt

1 cup all-purpose flour

4 large eggs

Classic Gruyère Gougères

¾ cup grated Gruyère cheese (about 4 ounces)

2 tablespoons minced fresh chives

½ teaspoon crushed black pepper

Olive and Parmesan Gougères

½ cup finely chopped pitted green or black olives (or a combination of the two)

½ cup grated Parmesan cheese

Fresh Herbs and Comté Gougères

½ cup finely chopped fresh herbs (a combination of chives, flat-leaf parsley, basil, marjoram or oregano, and thyme)

½ cup grated Comté cheese

Bacon and Emmenthal Gougères

⅓ cup finely diced and sautéed bacon or pancetta

⅔ cup grated Emmenthal or Swiss cheese

1 teaspoon Dijon mustard

continued

Position 1 rack in the upper third of the oven and 1 rack in the bottom third. Preheat oven to 400°F. Line 2 baking sheets with parchment paper.

In a medium saucepan, bring the water, butter, and salt to a simmer, whisking until butter melts (no need to let it come to a full boil). Lower the heat to medium, and then add the flour all at once. Stir quickly with a wooden spoon until the flour absorbs all the liquid and the dough forms a ball, pulling away from the sides of the pan (this should take 30-60 seconds). Keep stirring vigorously until a film forms on the bottom of the pan and dough is no longer sticky, 1-2 minutes. Remove from heat. Transfer the dough to the bowl of a stand mixer fitted with the paddle attachment, or to a large mixing bowl if using a hand mixer. Let the dough cool for 5 minutes, beating it for a few seconds every 1 minute to let some steam out of the dough.

Crack 1 egg into the bowl with the dough. Beat until the egg is incorporated, about 2 minutes. The dough will first look curdled, but then it will come back together. Repeat to add the remaining 3 eggs, making sure you fully incorporate each egg before adding the next. At the end of the process, the dough should be smooth, thick, and sticky. Use a spatula to fold in the flavor ingredients of your choice.

Using a mini cookie scoop, shape Gougères and set them 2 inches apart on the prepared baking sheets. If you don't have a cookie scoop, drop the dough by heaping teaspoonfuls on the parchment paper. The dough should be thick enough to keep its rounded shape. Using damp fingertips, pat down peaks of dough to create round puffs, if desired.

Set 1 baking sheet on each oven rack. Bake until golden brown, about 30 minutes, rotating the baking sheets halfway through. Using a small paring knife, pry open one gougère to check for doneness: the center should be slightly eggy and moist. Remove from oven and transfer to a wire rack. Allow to cool completely.

After cooling, store at room temperature in an airtight container for up to 12 hours, or refrigerate for up to 2 days. If desired, reheat in a 350°F oven for 5-10 minutes before serving.

MARINATED MUSHROOMS

Makes about 1½ cups

I like to keep a jar of these marinated mushrooms in the fridge at all times. The flavors continue to bloom as days pass, and they'll keep refrigerated for two weeks. Serve with Crunchy Seed Crackers (page 42) or toasted baguette slices (see page 74). Marinated mushrooms can also serve to dress up pasta or as a condiment for meats. Once you've eaten all the mushrooms, don't throw away the marinating oil. Use it to drizzle over salads or pasta.

½ pound mixed mushrooms, coarsely chopped

½ cup extra virgin olive oil

¼ cup chopped mixed fresh herbs (a combination of chives, marjoram or oregano, and flat-leaf parsley)

1 tablespoon finely grated lemon zest (about ½ lemon)

2 tablespoons freshly squeezed lemon juice (about 1 lemon)

2 tablespoons champagne vinegar, white balsamic vinegar, or white wine vinegar

2 cloves garlic, crushed with the side of a knife

½ teaspoon crushed coriander seeds

½ teaspoon crushed fennel seeds

½ teaspoon crushed black pepper

½ teaspoon kosher salt

Bring a pot of water to a boil. Add the mushrooms and blanch for 90 seconds. Drain and pat dry with paper towels.

In a mixing bowl, whisk together the oil, herbs, zest, juice, vinegar, garlic, coriander, fennel, pepper, and salt. Add the mushrooms and toss to coat. Transfer to an airtight jar. Let rest at room temperature for 2–3 hours for the flavors to infuse. Always bring the marinated mushrooms back to room temperature before serving (the olive oil will solidify upon refrigeration).

*See page 30 for photo.

CRUNCHY SEED CRACKERS

Makes about 48 crackers

I'm a huge cracker fan: you'll usually find four to five varieties in my pantry at all times. Whenever I can carve out the time, I bake a double batch of these crackers. They're as fun to make as playing with Play-Doh—get the kids involved! Filled with good-for-you ingredients, dairy free, and even gluten free if you substitute brown rice flour, these crackers are so good you will want to eat them like chips. Serve with any of the dips and spreads included in Basics and Condiments (page 12) or with Goat Cheese Truffles, Four Ways (page 32), Instant Fish Rillettes, Three Ways (page 34), or Marinated Mushrooms (page 41).

¼ cup pumpkin seeds

¼ cup sunflower seeds

2 tablespoons flaxseeds (whole or ground) or hemp seeds

1 cup whole-wheat flour

2 tablespoons chia seeds

2 tablespoons sesame seeds

1 teaspoon herbes de Provence (see page 28)

½ teaspoon baking soda

½ teaspoon kosher salt

¼ cup extra virgin olive oil

¼ cup water

Sea salt flakes, for sprinkling

In a food processor, combine the pumpkin seeds, sunflower seeds, and flaxseeds (if whole; if ground, stir in after pulsing). Pulse a few times to get a coarse texture. Transfer to a large mixing bowl. Add the flour, chia seeds, sesame seeds, herbes de Provence, baking soda, and salt; whisk to combine. Drizzle in the olive oil and water. Using a fork or pastry cutter, incorporate the liquids into the dry ingredients until fully combined and the texture resembles coarse meal.

Preheat oven to 350°F and line a baking sheet with parchment paper.

Transfer the dough to a lightly floured work surface, and use your hands to gather the dough into a disk. If the dough seems crumbly, add 1 or 2 tablespoons of water to help the dough stick together. The dough should hold together with a texture similar to Play-Doh.

Roll the dough to a ⅛-inch thickness. The dough will crack as you go, but you can simply pat it back together as you would Play-Doh. Lightly sprinkle the dough with more flour as needed. Using a cookie cutter, knife, or pizza cutter, cut dough into individual crackers that are about 2 inches in diameter. Transfer to the prepared baking sheet, setting the crackers very close to one another as they will not expand. Lightly spray or brush with olive oil then sprinkle with sea salt flakes. Bake for 20–25 minutes, until the edges of the crackers are lightly golden (the size and shape of the crackers will influence the baking time). Transfer to a wire rack and let cool completely before serving.

Store the crackers in an airtight container at room temperature for up to 1 month.

*See page 22 for photo.

PISTACHIO FALAFEL

Makes about 40 (1-inch) falafel

When I go to Paris, I make a point of eating at least once on rue des Rosiers, a street in the 4th arrondissement that is lined with Middle Eastern joints that sell thousands of fried chickpea bites every day. My falafel are baked, and I like to use a mini cookie scoop to shape them in a flash. You can bake and freeze falafel; simply reheat in a 325°F oven for 8–10 minutes before serving. Serve the falafel with Any-Bean Hummus (page 18) or Beet, Goat Cheese, and Orange Dip (page 25).

1 (15.5-ounce) can chickpeas, rinsed, drained, and patted dry

½ cup shelled, toasted pistachios

½ cup almond flour

¼ cup fresh mint leaves

¼ cup fresh flat-leaf parsley leaves

1 shallot, minced

1 teaspoon finely grated lemon zest

2 tablespoons freshly squeezed lemon juice (about ½ lemon)

3 tablespoons extra virgin olive oil

1 tablespoon all-purpose flour

1 teaspoon baking soda

1 teaspoon kosher salt

½ teaspoon cardamom powder

Freshly ground black pepper, to taste

Preheat oven to 400°F. Line a baking sheet with parchment paper.

In a food processor, add all the ingredients. Pulse, frequently scraping down the sides of the bowl, until you reach a coarse but uniform texture. Remove the bowl from the processor and pull out the blade. Using a mini cookie scoop or your hands, roll the falafel mixture into balls and set onto the baking sheet. Bake for 15–18 minutes, until the falafel are lightly golden and firm to the touch. Let cool for 10 minutes before serving; this will allow the falafel to firm up and reach their ideal texture.

45

CHICKEN AND OLIVE MEATBALLS

Makes about 40 (1-inch) meatballs

These lean meatballs combine ground chicken and olives in a small bite that begs to be dipped in one of my favorite three French condiments: Pistou (page 13), Aïoli (page 17), or Tapenade, Three Ways (page 14). Make sure to gently mix the ingredients and manipulate the mixture as little as possible when you shape the meatballs; this will ensure they remain tender and juicy after baking.

1 pound ground chicken or turkey

3 cloves garlic, minced

½ cup breadcrumbs

¼ cup oil-packed pitted black olives (such as Kalamata), drained and minced

1 teaspoon finely grated lemon zest

2 teaspoons herbes de Provence (see page 28)

1 teaspoon kosher salt

Freshly ground black pepper, to taste

Preheat oven to 400°F. Line a baking sheet with parchment paper.

In a large mixing bowl, add all the ingredients. Mix just until the flavorings are incorporated through the meat. Using a small cookie scoop or your hands, roll the mixture into balls and set onto the baking sheet. Bake until the meatballs are firm, about 12 minutes. If desired, broil for 1 minute to give them more color.

SAVORY SABLÉS, THREE WAYS

Each variation makes 40 sablés

My love for sweet sablés inspired the creation of these savory varieties. I can think of no better treat to enjoy with sparkling wine than these buttery, cheesy, nutty cookies. These elegant sablés are as easy to make as slice-and-bake cookies. They're best enjoyed in the first 24 hours after baking, so my tip is to stash rolls of dough in the freezer so you can bake them on demand.

Gruyère and Hazelnut Sablés

½ cup (4 ounces) butter, room temperature

1 egg, room temperature

2 ounces grated Gruyère cheese (about ½ cup)

½ cup chopped toasted hazelnuts

1 teaspoon finely grated orange zest

¼ teaspoon kosher salt

Freshly ground black pepper, to taste

1 cup all-purpose flour

Blue Cheese and Cherry Sablés

½ cup (4 ounces) salted butter, room temperature

1 egg, room temperature

2 ounces crumbled blue cheese (such as Roquefort; about ½ cup)

⅓ cup chopped dried cherries or cranberries

⅓ cup chopped walnuts

½ teaspoon chopped fresh rosemary

¼ teaspoon kosher salt

Freshly ground black pepper, to taste

1 cup all-purpose flour

Comté and Fig Sablés

½ cup (4 ounces) butter, room temperature

1 egg, room temperature

2 ounces grated Comté cheese (about ½ cup)

⅓ cup chopped dried figs

⅓ cup chopped walnuts

½ teaspoon crushed fennel seeds

¼ teaspoon kosher salt

Freshly ground black pepper, to taste

1 cup all-purpose flour

continued

In a large mixing bowl, beat the butter until creamy and smooth. Add all the ingredients of your choice except the flour and mix at low speed to incorporate. Add the flour all at once and mix just until no trace of flour remains.

Transfer the dough onto a work surface and use your hands to gather into a disk (the dough will be sticky). Cut into 2 equal portions of dough. Place 1 portion onto a large piece of plastic wrap to prevent the dough from sticking to both your work surface and your hands then shape into a thin log of about 1 inch in diameter and 10 inches in length. Wrap the log tightly into the plastic wrap, and repeat to shape the second log. Refrigerate for at least 2 hours, or up to 3 days. (You can also freeze the raw dough for up to 1 month.)

Preheat oven to 350°F. Line a baking sheet with parchment paper. Take the logs out of the refrigerator, unwrap, and then use a serrated knife to slice each log into 20 (½-inch-thick) cookies. Transfer the cookies to the prepared baking sheet, setting them about 1 inch apart. Bake until the edges begin to brown, 12–15 minutes, rotating the pan halfway through. Transfer the sablés to a wire rack and let cool completely.

The flavor and texture of sablés are at their best the day after they are made. Store sablés in an airtight container at room temperature for up to 3 days.

PALMIERS, THREE WAYS

These palmiers are the ace up your sleeve when company shows up unannounced. Sheets of frozen puff pastry thaw within 20 minutes at room temperature. Slather them with one of the delicious spreads included in this book, or use store-bought pesto or tapenade if you're short on time. However you decide to garnish them, I guarantee palmiers will always be the treat that disappears the fastest in your cocktail hour spread.

1 (1-pound) package store-bought puff pastry (preferably 100% butter), defrosted if frozen

Lemon Pistou Palmiers

½ cup Classic Pistou (made with Parmesan if desired; page 13)

1 tablespoon finely grated lemon zest (about 1 lemon)

Tapenade and Parmesan Palmiers

½ cup Tapenade of your choice (page 14)

½ cup finely grated Parmesan cheese

French Everything Palmiers

½ cup French Everything Flavoring Mix (page 28)

½ cup grated Comté or Gruyère cheese

Unroll 1 sheet of puff pastry onto a working surface, leaving it on the wrapping paper. Spread with half of the ingredients of your choice, making sure the full surface of the pastry is covered. If making the French Everything Palmiers, gently press the ingredients into the pastry so they hold better upon rolling; you can use a rolling pin to do this.

Starting from one of the long edges, tightly roll the pastry up to the center; repeat from the other side. Wrap the pastry in the wrapping paper, and then adjust the shape of the palmiers if needed. Repeat to prepare the second roll of pastry. Freeze the prepared pastry for 20 minutes, or refrigerate for up to 3 hours.

continued

Position 1 rack in the upper third of the oven and 1 rack in the bottom third. Preheat oven to 400°F. Line 2 baking sheets with parchment paper.

Lightly grease a very sharp knife and cut the prepared pastry into slices a bit thinner than ½ inch. Set the palmiers flat onto the prepared baking sheet, spacing 2 inches apart to allow them to expand.

Set 1 baking sheet on each oven rack. Bake the palmiers until crisp and golden, about 18 minutes, rotating the baking sheets halfway through. Transfer to a wire rack and let the palmiers cool to room temperature.

Palmiers are best enjoyed the day they are baked. Store leftover palmiers in an airtight container at room temperature for up to 2 days.

SAVORY CAKES AND TARTS

Gâteaux et tartes salés

Caramelized Fennel, Lemon, and Comté Cake

Zucchini, Cured Ham, and Goat Cheese Muffins

Cherry Tomato, Spinach, and Goat Cheese
Sheet Pan Quiche

Pear and Blue Cheese Savory Galette

Tapenade and Parmesan Madeleines

CARAMELIZED FENNEL, LEMON, AND COMTÉ CAKE

Makes 1 loaf cake

Cakes salés, or savory cakes, are an apéro staple in France. You can make them so many different ways, but I like mine cheesy and brimming with textured ingredients. This cake combines the complex sweetness of caramelized fennel with the zestiness of lemon and sharpness of Comté cheese. The flavors keep developing as the cake rests, which makes it even better the next day.

Caramelized Fennel

1 tablespoon extra virgin olive oil

1 medium fennel bulb (about 12 ounces), trimmed, cored, and thinly sliced

2 cloves garlic, minced

½ teaspoon granulated sugar

½ teaspoon kosher salt

Freshly ground black pepper, to taste

Cake

1½ cups all-purpose flour

2 teaspoons baking powder

1 teaspoon crushed fennel seeds

½ teaspoon kosher salt

4 eggs

½ cup extra virgin olive oil

1 teaspoon finely grated lemon zest (about ½ lemon)

2 tablespoons freshly squeezed lemon juice (about ½ lemon)

1 teaspoon whole grain or Dijon mustard

2 ounces grated Comté cheese (about ½ cup)

¼ cup chopped fresh flat-leaf parsley

continued

Caramelized Fennel In a skillet, heat the olive oil over medium-high heat. Add the fennel and stir to coat with oil. Add the garlic and sprinkle with the sugar, salt, and pepper. Cook, stirring from time to time, until fennel starts to brown, about 5 minutes. Reduce heat to low, cover the pan, and continue cooking for 10 minutes, stirring once or twice. Uncover and cook for 2–3 minutes more to evaporate leftover liquids, if any. Transfer to a bowl to cool.

Cake Preheat oven to 350°F. Grease a 9 x 5-inch loaf pan. Line the bottom and two longer sides of the pan with a sling of parchment paper.

In a large mixing bowl, whisk together the flour, baking powder, fennel seeds, and salt. In a second bowl, whisk together the eggs, olive oil, zest, juice, and mustard. Pour the mixture over the dry ingredients and stir until just combined. Fold in the caramelized fennel, cheese, and parsley. Transfer the batter to the prepared loaf pan. Use a spatula to smooth out the surface.

Bake until the bread is puffed and golden and a toothpick inserted in the center comes out clean, about 60 minutes. Remove from oven and let cool for 15 minutes. Pull on the parchment paper to unmold the bread, running a knife around the pan if necessary. Transfer to a wire rack and let cool completely.

Slice the bread into cubes and serve at room temperature, or warm in a 350°F oven for 10 minutes before serving.

*Note: The batter can also be baked in a standard muffin pan. Grease and line the pan with parchment paper liners. Divide the batter between the cups and bake for 25 minutes, or until the cupcakes are lightly golden.

ZUCCHINI, CURED HAM, AND GOAT CHEESE MUFFINS

Makes 12 cupcakes

These generously filled savory muffins are sturdy and universally loved, so I like to pack them for picnics and bring them to potlucks. They're at their very best warm, so make sure to gently reheat them before serving, if you can.

1 medium zucchini, grated (about 1 cup firmly packed)

1½ cups all-purpose flour

1 teaspoon baking powder

1 teaspoon coarsely ground black pepper

½ teaspoon kosher salt

3 eggs

¾ cup plain yogurt

¼ cup extra virgin olive oil

¼ cup minced fresh chives

3 ounces Bayonne ham (French dry-cured ham) or prosciutto, chopped, divided

About 4 ounces log-style goat cheese, crumbled

Freshly ground black pepper, to taste

Lay a double layer of paper towels on a plate. Scatter the zucchini over the towels. Cover with another paper towel, and then firmly press down on the zucchini to release excess water. Set aside to rest while you prepare the muffins.

Preheat the oven to 400°F. Line 12 muffin cups with paper liners.

In a large mixing bowl, whisk together the flour, baking powder, pepper, and salt. In a second bowl, whisk together the eggs, yogurt, olive oil, and chives. Pour the mixture over the dry ingredients and stir until just combined. Add the zucchini and ⅔ of the ham; stir just to incorporate. (Separate the pieces of ham as you add them to the batter so they don't stick together. You don't want to separate the ham once it's already in the batter, as it will lead to overstirring.)

Divide the mixture between the prepared muffin cups. Garnish with the remaining ham, and then sprinkle with the cheese. Season with pepper.

Bake for about 25 minutes, or until the muffins are set and golden brown on top. Transfer to a wire rack and let cool completely. Refrigerate in an airtight container for up to 2 days, or freeze for up to 1 month. Always return the muffins to room temperature before serving, or reheat them in a 300°F oven for 10 minutes.

Tip: You can divide the batter between mini muffin cups to create bite-size treats, baking for 15 minutes, or bake the whole thing in a single loaf pan for 60 minutes.

CHERRY TOMATO, SPINACH, AND GOAT CHEESE SHEET PAN QUICHE

Makes 1 (9 x 13-inch) quiche (about 18 bite-size servings)

Baking a big batch of mini quiches for a crowd is a lovely idea, but it's so much work! I prefer making one huge quiche, which I then slice into small squares to serve—the same taste for a fraction of the effort! This recipe requires you to make a double batch of Shortcrust Pastry to generously cover the whole sheet pan.

1 double batch Shortcrust Pastry (regular or whole wheat, page 26), wrapped in plastic wrap and refrigerated for 1 hour

8 eggs

¾ cup heavy cream

¾ cup milk

½ teaspoon kosher salt

Freshly ground black pepper, to taste

Cherry Tomato, Spinach, and Goat Cheese Topping

4 ounces baby spinach, chopped

¼ cup Classic Pistou (page 13)

¼ cup grated Parmesan cheese

¼ cup chopped fresh chives

½ pound cherry tomatoes, halved

4 ounces goat cheese

Take the shortcrust out of the refrigerator 20–30 minutes before rolling. Preheat the oven to 400°F. Lightly grease a 9 x 13-inch sheet pan and line with parchment paper.

On a lightly floured work surface, roll out the dough to a rectangle large enough to generously fit the sheet pan (about 14 x 18 inches). Sprinkle more flour over and under dough as you roll, if needed. To transfer dough to the pan, gently roll dough around your rolling pin and unroll it on the sheet pan. Using the tips of your fingers, ease dough into the corners. Trim overhanging dough, leaving a 1½-inch border all around. Tuck this excess dough under then crimp to create a thick border. Prick the bottom of the crust all over with a fork. Cover with a sheet of parchment paper and fill with pie weights, pushing them to the edges to make sure the borders will stay up.

Bake for 20 minutes, remove the parchment paper and weights, and bake for 5 minutes more. Set aside to cool. Leave the oven on to bake the quiche.

In a large mixing bowl, whisk the eggs, cream, milk, salt, and pepper. Set aside.

Stir the spinach, pistou, Parmesan, and chives into the quiche base. Pour the mixture into the parbaked crust, using a spatula to evenly distribute the filling ingredients. Dot the mixture with the cherry tomatoes and crumble the cheese all over. Bake for 25–30 minutes, until the filling is set and the top is golden brown. Transfer to a wire rack to cool.

To serve Slice the quiche into squares. Serve warm or at room temperature.

PEAR AND BLUE CHEESE SAVORY GALETTE

Makes 1 (12-inch) galette

I came up with this galette to indulge my love for dishes that combine savory and sweet flavors. Fruit galettes are such a lovely, rustic way to highlight seasonal fruits, which combine so well with rich French cheeses. This galette layers slowly caramelized onions, cheese, fruit, and nuts to create an elegant dish you'll want to serve from brunch to dinner.

1 batch Shortcrust Pastry (whole wheat, page 26)

1 tablespoon extra virgin olive oil

1 tablespoon butter

1 pound sweet onions (such as Vidalia), thinly sliced

½ teaspoon kosher salt

1 tablespoon water

1 tablespoon Dijon mustard

About 1 tablespoon milk

Sea salt flakes, for sprinkling

Pear and Blue Cheese Topping

½ cup crumbled blue cheese (such as Roquefort; about 2 ounces), divided

1 pound firm pears (such as Anjou or Bosc), cored and sliced

1 large handful arugula, for garnish

⅓ cup coarsely chopped toasted hazelnuts, for garnish

On a lightly floured work surface, roll the pastry out to a 15-inch circle. Transfer to a baking sheet (the edges can fold up if the pastry circle doesn't fit flat into the sheet) and refrigerate for 30 minutes.

Heat the olive oil and butter in a skillet set over medium heat. Add the onions, salt, and water; stir to coat. Reduce the heat to low, cover the pan, and cook until the onion is very soft, stirring from time to time, about 25 minutes. Uncover, increase the heat to medium high, and cook for 2–3 minutes more, stirring from time to time, to evaporate any leftover liquids. Transfer to a bowl to cool.

Preheat oven to 425°F. Take the crust out of the refrigerator. Spread with the mustard, leaving a 2-inch border all around, and evenly distribute the onion mixture over the top.

Sprinkle ¼ cup of the cheese over the onion. Top with the pear slices, fanning them in circles. Bring the edges of the dough up and over the filling, creasing it and gently pressing it down onto the filling as you go. Brush the dough with milk and sprinkle with sea salt. Bake for 30 minutes. Sprinkle with the remaining cheese and bake for 5 minutes more, or until the crust is golden brown. Transfer to a wire rack for 10 minutes. Garnish with arugula and hazelnuts and serve.

TAPENADE AND PARMESAN MADELEINES

Makes 24 regular madeleines or 40 mini madeleines

When I first started developing recipes for this book, I basically wanted to create a savory version of every French snack cake. Some of my experiments didn't go so well (I'm looking at you, savory financiers.), but madeleines were a raving success. You can make them ahead of time, even freeze them, and gently reheat before serving to return them to their freshly baked state.

¾ cup all-purpose flour

¼ cup finely grated Parmesan cheese

2 teaspoons baking powder

½ teaspoon kosher salt

¼ teaspoon baking soda

Freshly ground black pepper, to taste

3 eggs

1 tablespoon granulated sugar

¼ cup extra virgin olive oil

3 tablespoons Tapenade of your choice (page 14)

Sea salt flakes, for sprinkling

In a bowl, whisk together the flour, cheese, baking powder, salt, baking soda, and pepper; set aside.

In a large mixing bowl, beat the eggs and sugar together for 3 minutes, or until the eggs are pale and fluffy. Whisk in the olive oil and Tapenade. Using a spatula, add the reserved dry ingredients ⅓ at a time, folding between each addition until just incorporated. Cover the mixing bowl with plastic wrap and refrigerate the batter for 30 minutes to 1 hour, or up to overnight.

continued

Preheat the oven to 400°F. Lightly grease a madeleine mold with cooking spray; use a brush to make sure the oil gets into every nook and cranny. Sprinkle with flour then tap out the excess. Place the pan in the freezer for 10 minutes.

Take the prepared mold out of the freezer. Take the batter out of the fridge. Using a spatula, gently mix the stiff batter to loosen it up and to remove excess bubbles that may have formed while the batter was resting. Fill each shell-shaped cavity with about 2 heaping teaspoons of batter for regular madeleines, or 1 scant teaspoon for mini madeleines (the cavities should be about ⅔ full). Return the remaining batter to the fridge.

Bake until the madeleines are puffed and golden, about 12 minutes for regular madeleines or 8 minutes for mini madeleines. Unmold as soon as you take the madeleines out of the oven by turning the mold upside down. You may need to gently tap a corner of the pan on the work surface to loosen them. Gently coax uncooperative madeleines out with the tip of a butter knife.

To bake the remaining madeleines, run the mold under cold running water to make it easier to handle. Clean it, lightly grease and flour again, and return to the freezer for 10 minutes. Fill with more madeleine batter and bake as indicated.

Just before serving, sprinkle the shell side of the madeleines with a bit of sea salt. Serve warm or at room temperature. Madeleines are best served the day they are baked. Store leftovers in an airtight container at room temperature for up to 2 days, or freeze for up to 1 month. To return the madeleines to their freshly baked state, thaw to room temperature then warm in a 300°F oven for 6–8 minutes.

BREADS, SANDWICHES, AND TOASTS

Pains, sandwiches, et croûtons

Fig, Walnut, and Orange Fougasse

Fresh Herb Pissaladière

Croûtons pour l'apéro (Cocktail Hour Toasted Bites)

Baked Croque Monsieur Fingers

Brioche Croque Madame Bites

FIG, WALNUT, AND ORANGE FOUGASSE

Makes 1 (10-inch) loaf

What would *l'apéro* be without good bread? Have you ever considered making your own? Granted, this is a project that takes time—mostly hands off, as bread dough needs time to rise—but it's so worth it. Fougasse is a Provençal flatbread that is traditionally shaped like a leaf. I like to use a bit of whole-wheat flour for a rustic flavor and stuff the dough with lots of flavorings so every bite is a rewarding surprise.

1 teaspoon active dry yeast

1 teaspoon granulated sugar

¾ cup warm water (about 115°F)

2 tablespoons extra virgin olive oil

1 tablespoon freshly grated orange zest (about ½ orange)

1 teaspoon crushed fennel seeds

½ teaspoon kosher salt

1 cup whole-wheat flour

1 cup all-purpose flour, plus more as needed

6 dried figs, each chopped into eighths

¼ cup chopped walnuts

To bake

2 tablespoons extra virgin olive oil

1 teaspoon chopped fresh rosemary

Sea salt flakes

Stand mixer method Using the dough hook attachment, mix the yeast, sugar, and water together. Let set until foamy, about 10 minutes. Mix in olive oil, zest, fennel seeds, and salt. Add the whole-wheat flour and mix just to combine. Add the all-purpose flour and knead the dough for 6–8 minutes, stopping the mixer from time to time to scrape down the hook and the bowl. If the dough is very sticky and keeps creeping up the hook, add a bit of flour, 1 tablespoon at a time, until the dough stops sticking. (You shouldn't

continued

need to add more than ¼ cup additional flour.) By the end of the kneading process, the dough should come together in a ball and feel smooth to the touch. Transfer to a lightly oiled bowl, cover with plastic wrap, and let set in a warm, non-drafty place until double in size, about 1½ hours.

Hand method In a large bowl, stir together the yeast, sugar, and water. Let set until foamy, about 10 minutes. Stir in olive oil, zest, fennel seeds, and salt. Add the flours and mix until the ingredients come together in a craggy ball. Transfer the dough to a lightly floured work surface. Knead for 6 minutes, until the dough feels smooth. If the dough is very sticky, add a bit of flour, 1 tablespoon at a time, until the dough stops sticking. (You shouldn't need to add more than ¼ cup additional flour.) Transfer to a lightly oiled bowl, cover with plastic wrap, and let set in a warm, non-drafty place until double in size, about 1½ hours.

Line a baking sheet with parchment paper. Transfer the dough to a lightly floured work surface. Flatten dough slightly, sprinkle with the figs and walnuts, fold in half, and then knead to incorporate, about 1 minute. If figs and walnuts keep falling out of the dough, place them on top of the dough, fold in half, and keep kneading until they're evenly distributed. Transfer the dough to the prepared baking sheet; stretch and flatten into a 10-inch round. Use a sharp knife or kitchen shears to cut 4 long slits through the dough. Spread the slits wide so you can see the baking sheet through them. Cover with plastic wrap and let rest in a warm spot for 1 hour.

To bake Preheat oven to 450°F.

In a small bowl, combine olive oil and the rosemary. Uncover the fougasse, generously brush with rosemary oil, and then sprinkle with sea salt. Bake until the fougasse is puffed and golden brown, about 15 minutes. Transfer to a wire rack and let cool completely.

Serve the fougasse on a large plate, letting guests tear away pieces as they wish.

FRESH HERB PISSALADIÈRE

Makes 24 (3 x 3-inch) pieces

Here's another delightful Provençal bread that's perfect for a warm and sunny cocktail hour. Traditional pissaladière usually features whole anchovy fillets as topping, but after noticing that it intimidated some of my guests, I started slathering the dough with Anchoïade instead. The dressing provides the same salty, intriguingly umami-filled flavor, without the fishy look. Tiny niçoise olives can be tricky to find; you can use Spanish Arbequinas instead.

Dough

1 teaspoon active dry yeast

1 teaspoon granulated sugar

1¼ cups warm water (about 115°F)

¼ cup extra virgin olive oil

1 teaspoon kosher salt

3½ cups all-purpose flour, plus more as needed

Topping

1 tablespoon extra virgin olive oil, plus more for drizzling

1 tablespoon butter

3 pounds red onions, halved and thinly sliced

1 teaspoon kosher salt

Freshly ground black pepper, to taste

1 batch Anchoïade (page 24)

½ cup fresh herb leaves (a combination of oregano, marjoram, flat-leaf parsley, and thyme)

½ cup black olives (preferably small niçoise)

Stand mixer method Using the dough hook attachment, mix the yeast, sugar, and water together. Let set until foamy, about 10 minutes. Mix in the olive oil and salt. Add half of

continued

the flour and mix just to combine. Add the remaining flour and knead at medium-slow speed for 6–8 minutes, stopping the mixer from time to time to scrape down the hook and the bowl. If dough is very sticky and keeps creeping up the hook, add a bit of flour, 1 tablespoon at a time, until the dough stops sticking. (You shouldn't need to add more than ¼ cup additional flour.) By the end of the kneading process dough should come together

in a ball and feel smooth to the touch. Transfer to a lightly oiled bowl, cover with plastic wrap, and let set in a warm, non-drafty place until doubled in size, about 1½ hours.

Hand method In a large bowl, stir together the yeast, sugar, and water. Let set until foamy, about 10 minutes. Stir in the olive oil and salt; add the flour and mix until the ingredients come together in a craggy ball of dough. Transfer to a lightly floured surface. Knead for 8–10 minutes, until dough feels smooth. If dough is very sticky, add a bit of flour, 1 tablespoon at a time, until dough stops sticking. (You shouldn't need to add more than ¼ cup additional flour.) Transfer to a lightly oiled bowl, cover with plastic wrap, and let set in a warm, non-drafty place until doubled in size, about 1½ hours.

Topping While the dough rises, melt the olive oil and butter in a large pot set over medium heat. Add the onions and sprinkle with the salt and pepper; stir to coat the onions with oil. Reduce heat to low, cover, and cook, stirring from time to time, until the onions are very soft and starting to caramelize, about 25 minutes. Uncover and cook for 2–3 minutes more to evaporate any leftover liquids. Transfer to a bowl to cool.

Generously grease an 13 x 18-inch baking sheet (half sheet pan) with oil. Transfer the dough onto the sheet. Using your fingers, gently press the dough into the sheet, stretching it until it completely covers the baking sheet. Cover with plastic wrap and let the dough rise until almost doubled in size, about 1 hour more.

To bake Preheat oven to 500°F. Uncover the dough. Create indentations all over by pressing the tip of your fingers into the dough. Brush the whole surface (right up to the edges) with the Anchoïade. Scatter the onions over dough, leaving a 1-inch border all around. Bake until dough is golden brown around the edges, about 20 minutes. Remove from oven and let cool slightly, about 10 minutes. Scatter with the herbs and olives, drizzle with oil, and cut into squares. Serve immediately.

CROÛTONS POUR L'APÉRO (COCKTAIL HOUR TOASTED BITES)

Each variation makes about 48 bites

This "recipe" is more of an illustration of the infinite bites you can create when you have a few staples on hand. Using recipes from the Basics and Nibbles chapters as building blocks, you can create dozens of garnished *croûtons*—toasted baguette slices in French—in a flash. Croûtons are a great way to use up leftovers too. Start here, and then use your creativity to make your own flavors. Share your favorites on social media using #FrenchAppetizers so we can all get inspired!

Toasted baguette slices

> **1 baguette, cut into ½-inch-thick slices**
> **Extra virgin olive oil, for drizzling**
> **Sea salt flakes, to taste**

Preheat oven to 400°F.

Set the bread slices side by side on a baking sheet. Drizzle with the olive oil then lightly sprinkle with the salt. Toast for 6 minutes, turn the slices, and then toast for another 6 minutes. Set the baking sheet on a wire rack and let the slices cool completely. Store in an airtight bag or container until ready to use. Just before serving, place the slices on 1 large serving plate, or several smaller ones, and choose one or more of the flavor options to top.

Hummus, Avocado, and Pumpkin Seeds

2 ripe avocados

Juice of ½ lemon

2 cups Any-Bean Hummus (page 18)

½ cup toasted pumpkin seeds

Sea salt flakes, to taste

Freshly ground black pepper, to taste

Peel and pit the avocados, dice, and place in a small bowl. Drizzle with the juice and toss to coat. Spread the toasted baguette slices with the hummus, top with avocado, and then sprinkle with the pumpkin seeds. Season with salt and pepper.

Salmon Rillettes, Green Apple, and Cilantro

2 green apples (such as Granny Smith or Crispin)

Juice of ½ lemon

Salmon and Capers Rillettes (page 34)

Freshly ground black pepper, to taste

1 bunch cilantro, for garnish

Core the apples then thinly slice. Drizzle with the juice and toss to coat. Spread the toasted baguette slices with salmon rillettes, top with apple, sprinkle with pepper, and garnish with coriander leaves.

Roasted Red Pepper, Cannellini Beans, and Arugula

1 (15.5-ounce) can cannellini beans, drained, rinsed, and patted dry

2 tablespoons extra virgin olive oil

1 tablespoon freshly squeezed lemon juice

½ teaspoon kosher salt

Freshly ground black pepper, to taste

1 cup Roasted Red Pepper and Hazelnut Dip (page 23)

2 large handfuls arugula, for garnish

¼ cup toasted, peeled, and crushed hazelnuts, for garnish

Toss the cannellini beans with the olive oil, juice, salt, and some pepper. Spread the toasted baguette slices with the dip, top with dressed beans, and garnish with the arugula and hazelnuts.

continued

Buttered Radishes, Crab, and Chives

1 batch Warm Brown Butter Bourbon Radishes (page 37)

½ pound lump crabmeat

Freshly ground black pepper, to taste

¼ cup minced fresh chives

Divide the radishes among the toasted baguette slices. Top with crabmeat, and then drizzle with additional dressing from the radishes. Season with pepper and sprinkle with chives.

Pistou, Cured Ham, and Roasted Cherry Tomatoes

½ pound cherry tomatoes

1 tablespoon extra virgin olive oil

Sea salt flakes, to taste

Freshly ground black pepper, to taste

1 cup Classic Pistou (page 13)

About 4 ounces Bayonne ham (French dry-cured ham) or prosciutto

Preheat oven to 450°F. Line a baking sheet with parchment paper. Scatter the cherry tomatoes over the lined baking sheet; drizzle with the olive oil and toss to coat. Sprinkle with salt and pepper. Roast for about 15 minutes, or until the tomatoes are soft and lightly browned or charred in spots. Let cool completely.

Spread the toasted baguette slices with the pistou. Top with the ham and garnish with roasted tomatoes.

Marinated Mushrooms and Brie

About 8 ounces Brie cheese

1½ cups Marinated Mushrooms (page 41)

Freshly ground black pepper, to taste

Fresh thyme leaves, for garnish

Thinly slice the cheese. Top the toasted baguette slices with cheese. Add the Marinated Mushrooms, season with pepper, and garnish with the thyme.

BAKED CROQUE MONSIEUR FINGERS

Makes 18 fingers

A croque monsieur is a baked ham and cheese sandwich with additional cheese melted on top. Some people add béchamel sauce inside the sandwich for additional creaminess; in my version of the croque monsieur, I substitute eggplant caviar to add flavor and nutritional value to the dish. The sandwiches are assembled and baked in batches. Simply slice into pieces and serve to a hungry crowd.

5 ounces (about 1⅓ cups) grated Gruyère, Swiss, or Emmenthal cheese (or a combination), divided

¾ cup heavy cream

2 ounces grated Parmesan cheese

Freshly ground black pepper, to taste

1 loaf rustic bread (about 9 inches in diameter)

¾ cup Eggplant Caviar (page 20)

6 thin slices oven-roasted ham

Lightly grease a 9 x 13-inch baking dish. Set a rack in the upper third of the oven and preheat to 500°F.

Measure ½ cup of the Gruyère and place into a small bowl; set the remaining cheese aside. Add the cream, Parmesan, and a generous grinding of pepper to the bowl. Stir to combine and set aside.

Cut 6 (½-inch-thick) slices from the bread. Make sure they fit into the baking dish when set side by side in sandwiched pairs. Cut off the edges of the slices to make them fit, if needed. Lightly toast the bread slices, and then place 3 of the slices back into the bottom of the prepared baking dish. Slather these slices with half of the Eggplant

Caviar then top each with 2 slices of ham, folding the ham to fit if required. Sprinkle with the reserved grated Gruyère. Slather the underside of the remaining slices of bread with the remaining Eggplant Caviar. Place these slices caviar side down over the cheese-topped bottom slices. Spoon the cheese and cream mixture over the sandwiches.

Bake for 12 minutes, until the croque monsieurs are bubbling and the cheese is golden brown. (You can broil the sandwiches to add more color if desired.) Remove from oven and set on a wire rack. Let cool for 20 minutes. Use a spatula to carefully remove the croque monsieurs from the baking dish, and then cut each sandwich into fingers. Transfer to a serving plate and enjoy.

BRIOCHE CROQUE MADAME BITES

Makes 12 bites

A croque madame is quite simply a croque monsieur with an added fried egg on top. In this recipe, I had fun minifying the dish into cute bites topped with fried quail eggs. Assembling the sandwiches with chic ingredients such as *Jambon de Bayonne* (Bayonne ham) and brioche bread makes this appetizer worthy of special occasions. To create the fanciest bites, you'll need to cut off the crusts and trim the eggs into perfect rounds, but don't throw anything away: the trimmings make a delicious snack.

4 ounces (about 1 cup) grated Gruyère, Swiss, or Emmenthal cheese (or a combination), divided

½ cup heavy cream

Freshly ground black pepper, to taste

6 thin slices brioche bread

Butter, room temperature, for spreading and frying

2 tablespoons Dijon mustard, divided

6 thin slices Bayonne ham (French dry-cured ham) or prosciutto

12 quail eggs

Salt, to taste

Lightly grease a baking sheet. Set a rack in the upper third of the oven and preheat to 425°F.

Measure approximately ⅔ of the cheese and place into a small bowl; set the remaining cheese aside. Add the cream to the bowl with a generous grinding of pepper. Stir to combine and set aside.

Spread both sides of the brioche slices with butter. Set a large skillet over medium

continued

heat. Toast the slices on both sides until golden brown. Transfer to a working surface, setting the slices in pairs, side by side. Slather each slice with 1 teaspoon Dijon mustard. Add half of the cheese and cream mixture, then add 2 slices of cured ham, and end with the remaining cheese and cream mixture on 3 of the slices. Close the sandwiches and top with the reserved grated cheese, making sure to fully cover the surface of the bread (this will prevent it from burning in the oven). Transfer the sandwiches to the prepared baking sheet.

Bake for 8–10 minutes, until the croque madames are bubbling and the cheese is golden brown. Remove from the oven and set on a wire rack. Let cool while you fry the eggs. (You can prepare the sandwiches in advance, cool them completely, and refrigerate in an airtight container. Reheat in a 350°F oven for 10 minutes just before serving.)

In a medium skillet over medium heat, melt 1 tablespoon of butter. Crack only the number of quail eggs in the pan that can fry without touching each other, about 4 to 6, and sprinkle with salt and pepper. Cook until the whites are just set, about 1 minute. Carefully transfer the eggs to a large plate, and then wipe the skillet clean with a paper towel. Melt 1 more tablespoon of butter and fry the remaining eggs.

Cut the crusts off the croque madames (keep them for later nibbling), and then slice each sandwich into 4 squares. Top each square with a quail egg. Transfer the bites to a plate and serve.

VERRINES

Verrines

Cherry Tomato, Strawberry, and Basil Gazpacho

Cauliflower and Apple Velouté

Carrot, Pistachio, and Hummus Verrine

Beef Tartare and Marinated Mushroom Verrine

CHERRY TOMATO, STRAWBERRY, AND BASIL GAZPACHO

Makes 4 cups

This cold soup is versatile and a perfect showcase for summer produce. In this recipe, I roast cherry tomatoes and strawberries with shallots and garlic, both to combine and to concentrate their flavors. Get this step done in advance and blend the whole soup later. Just remember that you need to refrigerate the soup before serving. This recipe makes enough for 12 small servings or 6 regular servings.

1 pound cherry tomatoes, halved

1 pound strawberries, hulled and quartered

1 shallot, sliced

3 cloves garlic, unpeeled

4 tablespoons extra virgin olive oil, divided

½ English cucumber, peeled and chopped

¾ cup water, plus more as needed

1 tablespoon white balsamic vinegar

1 teaspoon kosher salt

½ teaspoon sambal oelek (chili paste, or substitute another hot sauce)

10 large fresh basil leaves, plus more to garnish

Preheat oven to 425°F. Line a baking sheet with parchment paper. Spread the tomatoes, strawberries, shallot, and garlic over the prepared baking sheet. Drizzle with 2 tablespoons olive oil and toss to coat. Roast for 35 minutes, or until the fruits are charred in spots. Let cool completely. (This step can be done up to a day in advance. Refrigerate in an airtight container until ready to use.)

Press the garlic cloves to extract the flesh. Discard the skins. Transfer the tomato and strawberry mixture to a blender and add the garlic, cucumber, water, remaining olive oil, vinegar, salt, sambal oelek, and basil. Blend until very smooth. Adjust the consistency to your liking by adding more water. Taste and adjust seasoning if needed. Transfer to an airtight container and refrigerate for at least 2 hours, or overnight, to let the flavors infuse.

Serve cool, garnished with additional basil.

CAULIFLOWER AND APPLE VELOUTÉ

Makes 6 cups

This silky-smooth soup is great on its own, but I like to use it as a canvas for garnishes. It is especially good when topped with luxurious seafood, such as lobster or crab. Adding more garnishes, such as diced apple and fresh herbs, elevates the presentation even further. This recipe makes enough for 18 small servings or 8 regular servings.

Soup

1 tablespoon butter

1 tablespoon extra virgin olive oil

1 leek, white part only, sliced

3 cloves garlic, minced

1 head cauliflower, cut into small florets

3 sweet apples (such as Golden Delicious or McIntosh), peeled, cored, and diced

4 cups vegetable broth

4 sprigs fresh thyme

½ teaspoon kosher salt

¼ teaspoon freshly grated nutmeg

½ cup heavy cream

To serve

1 apple (same variety used in the soup)

1 teaspoon freshly squeezed lemon juice

Fresh thyme leaves

1 cup cooked crabmeat, shrimp, or lobster, shredded or cut into small pieces (optional)

In a large pot set over medium heat, melt the butter into the olive oil. Add the leek and cook until softened, about 3 minutes. Add the garlic and cook for 1 minute more. Add the cauliflower, apples, broth, thyme, salt, and nutmeg. Bring to a boil, half cover, and simmer for 25 minutes, or until the cauliflower is very soft. Remove the thyme from the soup. Use a blender to process the soup to a very smooth consistency. Return to the pot and stir in the cream. Taste and adjust seasoning if needed.

You can serve this soup either warm or cold. If serving cold, store the puréed soup in an airtight container and refrigerate until cool, at least 3 hours. If serving warm, reheat the soup just before serving.

To serve, core the apple and cut into matchsticks; drizzle with lemon juice to prevent browning. Divide the soup between serving glasses or bowls, and garnish with apple matchsticks, thyme leaves, and crabmeat.

CARROT, PISTACHIO, AND HUMMUS VERRINE

For 8 verrines

I created this recipe to highlight a quintessential French salad: *carottes râpées*, or grated carrots. This super simple salad combines thin strands of carrots with olive oil, lemon juice, salt, and pepper. You can use a food processor, a mandoline, or the shredder attachment of a stand mixer to achieve those thin carrot strands. You can also look in the produce section of your supermarket: you're likely to find packages of shredded carrots alongside coleslaw mixes.

Carrot Salad

3 medium carrots (about 6.5 ounces), finely grated

¼ cup freshly squeezed lemon juice (about 1 lemon)

2 tablespoons extra virgin olive oil

½ teaspoon granulated sugar

½ teaspoon kosher salt

Freshly ground black pepper, to taste

2 tablespoons minced flat-leaf parsley

To serve

2 cups Any-Bean Hummus (page 18)

⅓ cup crushed pistachios

Microgreens

Sea salt flakes

Freshly ground black pepper

In a mixing bowl, combine all the carrot salad ingredients. Let rest for 10 minutes.

To assemble the verrines, add ¼ cup hummus to each of 8 small serving glasses. Add a generous ¼ cup of the carrot salad, and then sprinkle with about 2 teaspoons crushed pistachios.

To serve, garnish with microgreens, a pinch of sea salt flakes, and some pepper. Serve immediately.

BEEF TARTARE AND MARINATED MUSHROOM VERRINE

Makes 8 verrines

Steak tartare is a classic French bistro dish that I wanted to celebrate in this colorful, luxurious verrine. You will want to buy the freshest, best quality of beef you can afford to make this dish, and then go the extra mile by making your own mayonnaise using very fresh eggs and best-quality oils. These elements will combine to create an outstanding foundation for the dish, over which you'll build texture—the secret of a tartare that delights everyone.

½ pound fresh, tender beef steak (such as filet mignon, tenderloin, or sirloin)

2 tablespoons minced fresh chives

½ teaspoon sea salt flakes

¼ teaspoon crushed red pepper

1½ cups Marinated Mushrooms (page 41), prepared at least 24 hours in advance

¼ cup Classic Mayo (page 16), or ¼ cup store-bought mayonnaise combined with 1 tablespoon freshly squeezed lemon juice

½ cup fresh herb leaves (a combination of marjoram or oregano, basil, and flat-leaf parsley), divided

¼ cup toasted, peeled, and crushed hazelnuts (see page 104)

Using a very sharp knife, finely dice the beef and transfer to a mixing bowl. Add the chives, salt, red pepper, and 2 tablespoons of the mushrooms' marinating liquid. Stir to combine and refrigerate for 30 minutes.

To assemble the verrines, divide the beef between 8 small serving glasses. Drop 1 rounded teaspoon mayo over the beef. Divide ¼ cup of the herbs evenly among each glass. Top each portion with 2 rounded tablespoons of mushrooms. Garnish with the remaining ¼ cup herbs and the hazelnuts. Serve immediately.

SWEET BITES

Bouchées sucrées

Spiced Madeleines with Salted Caramel Sauce

Roasted Fig and Aniseed Financiers

Chamomile Lemon Tartlets

Cherry Clafoutis Bars

Chocolate and Tahini Sablés

Strawberry-Lemon Yogurt Sheet Cake

Berry Cups with Green Tea and Honey Syrup

Triple Lemon Dark Chocolate Truffles

Salted Butter Caramels

SPICED MADELEINES WITH SALTED CARAMEL SAUCE

Makes 36 regular madeleines or 72 mini madeleines

As simple as madeleines are to make, they always create a big impression. Their delicate shell shape is a conversation starter, and their tender, airy crumb is memorable. Making classic madeleines requires a specialty baking pan, but it would be completely acceptable to bake this spiced batter in muffin pans. If you do, only fill the prepared cups one-third of the way up to create thin cakes with delightfully crisp edges that mimic the original treat. One last note: Keep the recipe for that Salted Caramel Sauce on hand because you'll want to make it again and again.

Salted Caramel Sauce

¼ cup water

¼ cup sugar

½ cup heavy cream, divided

1 tablespoon unsalted butter

Scraped seeds from ½ vanilla bean, 1 teaspoon vanilla bean paste, or 2 teaspoons pure vanilla extract

1/2 teaspoon sea salt (such as fleur de sel flakes or another smooth-tasting sea salt)

Madeleines

1 cup all-purpose flour

1 teaspoon baking powder

½ teaspoon ground cinnamon

½ teaspoon ground cardamom

¼ teaspoon allspice

¼ teaspoon freshly grated nutmeg

Pinch of kosher salt

3 eggs

⅔ cup granulated sugar

1 tablespoon finely grated orange zest (about ½ orange)

1 teaspoon pure vanilla extract

½ cup unsalted butter, melted and cooled to room temperature (plus more for buttering the madeleine pan)

continued

Salted Caramel Sauce Add the water and sugar to a medium stainless steel saucepan. Set pan over medium heat and stir until the sugar fully melts. Bring the mixture to a boil and let it roll, gently swirling the pan from time to time, until the sugar turns to a beautiful amber color. Remove from heat then whisk in ¼ cup of the cream. (Be careful as the mixture will release hot steam and bubble up significantly.) Return pan to the heat and bring back to a boil, whisking constantly. Whisk in the butter, vanilla, and salt, then stir in the remaining cream. Cook for 2 minutes, until thickened and smooth. Strain through a fine-mesh strainer into a glass jar. Serve immediately or refrigerate in an airtight jar for up to 1 week. Rewarm before serving.

Madeleines In a bowl, whisk together the flour, baking powder, cinnamon, cardamom, allspice, nutmeg, and salt; set aside.

In a large mixing bowl, beat the eggs and sugar together for 3 minutes, or until the eggs are pale and fluffy. Mix in the zest and vanilla. With the mixer running at slow speed, drizzle the butter into the batter, mixing just to incorporate. Using a spatula, add the reserved dry ingredients, ⅓ at a time, folding between each addition until just incorporated. Cover the bowl with plastic wrap and refrigerate the batter for 30 minutes to 1 hour, or up to overnight.

Preheat oven to 400°F. Brush a madeleine mold with butter, making sure the butter gets into every nook and cranny. Sprinkle the pan with flour and shake off the excess. Place the pan in the freezer for 10 minutes.

Take the prepared madeleine mold out of the freezer. Take the batter out of the refrigerator. Using a spatula, gently mix the batter to relax it and remove excess bubbles that may have formed while resting. Fill each shell-shaped cavity with about 2 heaping teaspoons of batter for regular madeleines, or a scant 1 teaspoon for mini madeleines (the cavities should be about ⅔ full). Return the remaining batter to the refrigerator.

Bake regular madeleines for 12 minutes or mini madeleines for 8 minutes, or until puffed and golden. Unmold as soon as you take the madeleines out of the oven by turning the mold upside down and tapping an edge of the pan against the working surface. Gently coax uncooperative madeleines out with the tip of a butter knife.

To bake the remaining madeleines, clean the pan, lightly grease and flour again, return to the freezer for 10 minutes, fill with more batter, and bake as indicated.

Serve the madeleines warm or room temperature with Salted Caramel Sauce on the side. Madeleines are best served the day they are baked. Store leftovers in an airtight container at room temperature for up to 2 days, or freeze for up to 1 month. To return the madeleines to their freshly baked state, bring to room temperature before warming in a 300°F oven for 6–8 minutes.

ROASTED FIG AND ANISEED FINANCIERS

Makes 24 financiers

Financiers are my favorite French cakes to make because they are so incredibly easy and versatile. I infused this version with a quintessential southern France spice: aniseed. If you don't like licorice, fear not. Aniseeds have a lovely fruity flavor that's subtler than fennel seeds and far removed from the pungent flavor you've probably tasted in black-colored candies. Financiers are traditionally made in small, rectangular-shaped molds, making them look like tiny gold bars—hence the name.

Roasted figs*

6 plump fresh figs

2 tablespoons granulated sugar

1 teaspoon pastis (optional)

Financiers

½ cup unsalted butter

1 cup almond flour (lightly spooned into the cup—do not pack)

½ cup all-purpose flour

½ cup granulated sugar

½ cup firmly packed brown sugar

¾ teaspoon crushed aniseeds

½ teaspoon baking powder

4 large egg whites, or ½ cup boxed egg whites

Roasted figs Preheat oven to 400°F. Line a baking sheet with parchment paper. Quarter the figs and place into a bowl. Sprinkle with sugar, drizzle with pastis, and gently mix to combine. Spread the figs over the prepared baking sheet, making sure to brush any leftover sugar and pastis over the figs. Roast for 20–25 minutes, until the figs are soft. Set aside to cool while you prepare the financiers.

continued

Financier: Reduce heat to 350°F. Line the cups of 2 muffin pans with parchment paper cups (financiers tend to stick to regular paper cups). You can also bake the financiers in 2 batches if you have only 1 muffin pan.

In a medium stainless steel saucepan or skillet over medium-high heat, heat the butter until completely melted and bubbly. Reduce heat to medium and keep simmering, swirling the pot from time to time. If the butter bubbles up, preventing you from seeing the color changing, lift the pot from the heat for a few seconds until the bubbles recede; return the pot to the heat. The butter is ready when the milk solids at the bottom of the pot turn brown and the butter gives off a nutty aroma. Pour the brown butter into a bowl, making sure to scrape all the caramelized bits, and let cool while you prepare the batter.

In a large mixing bowl, whisk the flours, sugars, aniseeds, and baking powder together. Add the egg whites and whisk until they are fully incorporated. The mixture will be thick and sticky. Whisk in the brown butter. At this point, the dough can be stored in an airtight container in the refrigerator for up to 2 days.

When ready to bake the financiers, drop 1 tablespoon of batter into each prepared muffin cup. Set 1 piece of fig onto each financier. Bake for about 12 minutes, rotating the pan halfway through, until the financiers are golden brown on the edges. Let cool for 10 minutes in the pan, and then transfer to a wire rack to cool completely.

Financiers are at their very best the day they're baked. Store leftover financiers in an airtight container at room temperature for up to 2 days. To return the financiers to their freshly baked state, warm in a 300°F oven for 6–8 minutes; let cool before serving.

*If you can't find fresh figs, you can replace the roasted figs with dried figs. Look for "soft dried figs," which have a rich, soft texture that closely resembles that of roasted figs.

CHAMOMILE LEMON TARTLETS

Makes 18 tartlets or 1 (9-inch) tart

Citrus fruits are my go-to ingredient when I want to bake a dessert. I like that citrus-based desserts tend to be less sweet, which makes them great palate cleansers. These tartlets are no exception. Inspired by the classic French lemon tart—which isn't topped with fluffy meringue—they have a mellower citrus flavor thanks to the chamomile-infused cream. Making individual tartlets creates a showstopping dessert, but if you're short on time, you can also bake the crust and filling in a single tart pan.

Chamomile Lemon Cream

1 cup heavy cream

½ cup granulated sugar

2 tablespoons dried chamomile flowers, crushed, or 2 best-quality chamomile tea bags, contents reserved and bags discarded

1½ tablespoons finely grated lemon zest (about 1½ lemons)

3 eggs

½ cup strained freshly squeezed lemon juice (about 2 lemons)

Crusts

1 batch Shortcrust Pastry (sweet, page 26)

To serve

Powdered sugar

Dried chamomile flowers (optional)

Chamomile Lemon Cream In a medium saucepan, whisk together the cream and sugar. Place over medium heat and stir to melt the sugar completely. Bring just to a

continued

simmer then turn off the heat. Stir in the chamomile and lemon zest, cover, and let steep for 20 minutes.

Strain the cream (if using chamomile from tea bags, strain through cheesecloth). Refrigerate for 1 hour, until cool. (You'll add the eggs and lemon juice just before filling the crusts.)

Crusts Preheat oven to 350°F. Lightly grease 2 (12-cup) muffin pans. (You can bake the tartlets in 2 batches if you have only 1 muffin pan.) Roll out the pastry to a ¼-inch thickness. Cut out 18 (3½-inch) rounds. Gently ease 1 pastry round into each of the muffin cups. Using a fork, prick the base of each tartlet several times. Place a paper muffin cup into each crust and add dried beans or pie weights. Bake the crusts for 12 minutes. Remove the paper cups and bake for 8 minutes more, or until the crusts are lightly golden. Lower the oven temperature to 300°F.

To assemble Pour the chamomile lemon cream into a large mixing bowl. Whisk in the eggs then the lemon juice. Divide the filling between the tartlet crusts.

Bake for about 16 minutes, or until the filling is set but still jiggly in the center (the filling will finish setting as the tartlets cool). Transfer to a wire rack and let cool completely. To unmold the tartlets, carefully slide the tip of a butter knife or a small pastry spatula in between the side of a tartlet and the pan and lift. Transfer the tartlets to a plate.

To serve, sprinkle with powdered sugar and garnish with chamomile flowers for an added flavor boost.

CHERRY CLAFOUTIS BARS

Makes 25 squares

I came up with this recipe because I wanted to create a portable version of one of my favorite summer desserts: cherry clafoutis. Cherries and hazelnuts are a match made in heaven, and adding brown butter to the mix—or *beurre noisette,* as it is called in French—creates a downright dreamy dessert. The texture of these bars is close to that of a blondie with juicy, delicious cherries dotted throughout.

Crust

½ cup toasted and peeled hazelnuts*

½ cup all-purpose flour

¼ cup granulated sugar

Pinch of kosher salt

¼ cup unsalted butter, melted

Filling

1 pound fresh cherries

½ cup unsalted butter

½ cup granulated sugar

2 eggs

½ cup all-purpose flour, sifted

Pinch of kosher salt

¼ cup heavy cream

2 teaspoons finely grated lemon zest (about 1 lemon)

1 teaspoon pure vanilla extract

¼ cup toasted, peeled, and crushed hazelnuts (see page 104)

Crust Preheat oven to 350°F. Grease an 8 x 8-inch baking pan with cooking spray. Line with parchment paper, letting two sides overhang. (This will make it easier to unmold the bars.)

In the bowl of a food processor, add the hazelnuts, flour, sugar, and salt. Process until the nuts are finely ground. Transfer to a medium bowl, drizzle in the melted butter, and mix until the ingredients are wet. Transfer to the prepared baking pan. Press the mixture down into the bottom of the pan, going all the way to the edges, to form the crust (the crust will be thin). Bake until golden all over, about 18 minutes. Remove from the oven and set on a wire rack while you prepare the filling. (Keep the oven on.)

Filling Use a cherry pitter to pit the cherries, or do it by hand; set the pitted cherries aside. Heat the butter in a medium stainless steel saucepan over medium-high heat until completely melted and bubbly. Lower the heat to medium and keep simmering, swirling the pot from time to time. If the butter bubbles up, preventing you from seeing the color changing, lift the pot from the heat for a few seconds until the bubbles recede; return the pot to the heat. The butter is ready when the milk solids at the bottom of the pot turn brown and the butter gives off a nutty aroma. Pour the brown butter into a bowl, making sure to scrape all the caramelized bits, and let cool while you prepare the rest of the filling.

In a medium mixing bowl, whisk the sugar and eggs together. Gradually whisk in the flour to make sure there are no lumps. Whisk in the salt, cream, zest, vanilla, and brown butter. (The batter will be thick.)

To assemble Distribute the cherries over the crust. Pour the clafoutis mixture over the cherries and use a spatula to spread it all over. Sprinkle with the crushed hazelnuts. Bake for 35–40 minutes, until the clafoutis is puffed and set in the center and golden brown around the edges. Transfer the pan to a wire rack and let cool completely. Refrigerate for 2 hours.

To serve, run a sharp knife along the two sides that are not covered by parchment paper. Pull on the parchment paper to lift the bars out of the pan. Use a very sharp knife to cut the bars into squares, making a gentle sawing motion to cut through

continued

the cherries without smashing them. Store the bars in an open container at room temperature for up to 1 day (storing them in a closed container will soften the bars more quickly), or in an airtight container in the refrigerator for up to 3 days.

*To toast and peel hazelnuts, spread the nuts over a baking sheet and place in a preheated 350°F oven for 15 minutes, shaking the tray every 5 minutes. When the skins are shiny and crackled, remove from the oven and transfer to a clean dish towel. Close the towel up into a bundle and rub the hazelnuts against one another vigorously to remove the skin. Open the towel and pick up the peeled hazelnuts. Discard the skins. Keep the peeled hazelnuts in an airtight container in the refrigerator until ready to use.

CHOCOLATE AND TAHINI SABLÉS

Makes 36 sablés

I can hardly think of a better treat to go with coffee or tea than buttery sablés. Sablés are simple slice-and-bake cookies with a flavor and texture that can be truly revelatory when you use the best ingredients to make them. These sablés have an exotic profile thanks to the combination of chocolate, tahini, and toasted sesame seeds, and are best enjoyed within a couple of days of baking. Only slice and bake the number of sablés you want and freeze the remaining dough until needed.

1¾ cups all-purpose flour

¼ cup cocoa powder

1 teaspoon kosher salt

2 ounces grated or very finely chopped dark chocolate

½ cup (1 stick) unsalted butter, room temperature

½ cup tahini (stir well before using)

½ cup granulated sugar

¼ cup powdered sugar

1 egg, lightly beaten

To serve

6 ounces chopped dark chocolate

Toasted sesame seeds

In a large bowl, sift together the flour, cocoa powder, and salt. Whisk to combine then whisk in the grated chocolate. Set aside.

In a large mixing bowl, beat the butter and tahini until smooth, about 3 minutes. Add the sugars and beat on low speed until the mixture is smooth and creamy, about 3 minutes. Add the egg and beat for 1 minute more. Add the flour mixture all at once and stir at low speed just to incorporate. (Avoid overworking the dough.)

continued

Transfer the dough to a work surface and gather it with your hands, pressing it down a few times to roughly shape into a disk. Cut into 2 equal portions. Place 1 portion onto a large piece of plastic wrap to prevent the dough from sticking to both your work surface and your hands, and then shape it into a thin log of about 1½ inches in diameter. Wrap the log tightly into the plastic wrap; repeat to shape the second log. Refrigerate for 3 hours, or up to 3 days. (You can also freeze the raw dough for up to 1 month.)

Preheat oven to 350°F. Line a baking sheet with parchment paper.

Take 1 log out of the refrigerator, unwrap, and use a serrated knife to slice into ⅓-inch-thick cookies. Transfer the cookies to the prepared baking sheet, setting them 1 inch apart. Bake for 18 minutes. Remove from the oven and let cookies cool on the sheet for 10 minutes. Transfer to a wire rack to cool completely. Repeat to bake the second batch of cookies, if desired.

To serve, gently melt the chocolate in the microwave or in a double-boiler. Spoon some chocolate over the sablés, or dip into the chocolate, and then sprinkle with the sesame seeds. Let cool until the chocolate sets.

Store leftover sablés in an airtight container at room temperature for up to 2 days.

STRAWBERRY-LEMON YOGURT SHEET CAKE

Makes 20 cake squares

Yogurt cake is a treat many French children grow up eating. It's often the first dessert they bake on their own because the ingredients in classic recipes are measured with the container of the yogurt used in the batter, an easy tool for children to use. My version comes together just as easily and creates a large cake that can feed a crowd. If it's not strawberry season, don't hesitate to dot the top of this cake with raspberries, blueberries, or even sliced apricots.

1½ cups all-purpose flour

2 teaspoons baking powder

¼ teaspoon kosher salt

1 cup granulated sugar

2 tablespoons finely grated lemon zest (about 2 lemons)

½ cup plain yogurt

½ cup extra virgin olive oil

1 teaspoon pure vanilla extract

3 eggs

½ pound strawberries, hulled and quartered

Whipped cream, for serving

Preheat oven to 350°F. Lightly grease a 9 x 13-inch baking dish. Line with parchment paper, letting two sides overhang. (This will make it easier to unmold the cake.)

In a mixing bowl, sift the flour, baking powder, and salt together; whisk to combine. In a second mixing bowl, combine the sugar and lemon zest; rub the two together using the back of a spoon or the tip of your fingers to thoroughly infuse the lemon flavor into the sugar. Add the yogurt, olive oil, and vanilla; whisk to combine. Add the eggs, 1 at a time, whisking well between each addition. Add the flour mixture and stir just to incorporate.

Transfer the batter to the prepared baking dish. Sprinkle with the strawberries. Bake for about 30 minutes, or until the cake is golden, set, and a toothpick inserted into the center comes out clean. Transfer to a wire rack and let cool completely.

To serve, run a sharp knife along the two sides that are not covered by parchment paper. Pull on the parchment paper to lift the cake out of the pan. Cut into 20 squares. Top each square with a dollop of whipped cream and serve.

Refrigerate leftover cake in an airtight container for up to 2 days. This cake does not freeze well because the strawberries turn watery upon thawing. Always return to room temperature before serving.

BERRY CUPS WITH GREEN TEA AND HONEY SYRUP

Serves 8

Here's a light, fresh dessert for the height of the summer season. It's super simple to assemble. You should prepare the syrup in advance to cool it fully before using. To serve, all you need to do is place gorgeous berries in small serving bowls and pour the green tea–infused syrup over them. Decorate with edible flowers if you can get your hands on them to make the dessert look truly special.

1½ cups water

3 tablespoons or 3 bags of top-quality Japanese green tea leaves

¼ cup honey

4 cups mixed berries (a combination of strawberries, blueberries, blackberries, and cherries), sliced into bite-size pieces

To serve

Edible flowers (optional)

Crushed pistachios

Bring the water to a boil. Add the green tea and steep for 10 minutes. Strain the tea then stir in the honey. Reheat the tea slightly to help fully dissolve the honey, if needed. Transfer to an airtight jar and let cool completely. Refrigerate until cool, at least 2 hours. (You can make the syrup up to 3 days in advance.)

Divide the berries between 8 small bowls or glasses. Generously pour the syrup over top. Garnish with edible flowers and pistachios. Serve immediately.

TRIPLE LEMON
DARK CHOCOLATE TRUFFLES

Makes 72 (¾-inch) square truffles

Most nights, I like to end my meal with a square of dark chocolate. For special occasions, I like to make my own truffles, which are great to share with guests. This is a simple recipe that requires you to use the best chocolate you can afford to ensure that you create a top-quality treat. Preserved lemon adds a delightful savory touch to the truffles, but if you don't have it on hand, you can sprinkle the truffles with flaky sea salt instead.

Candied Lemon Zest

1 lemon, well-scrubbed

½ cup water

½ cup granulated sugar, plus more for dusting

Truffles

8 ounces dark chocolate, finely chopped

⅓ cup heavy cream

1 tablespoon preserved lemon rind

2 teaspoons finely grated lemon zest (about 1 lemon)

Candied Lemon Zest Using a vegetable peeler, peel the lemon, being careful to leave as much white pith behind as you can. Thinly slice the lemon strips. Fill a small saucepan with cold water and add the strips. Bring to a boil then drain. Fill the saucepan with cold water again, add the lemon strips, and bring to a boil. Drain the strips and set aside.

Add the ½ cup water and sugar to the saucepan and place over medium-high heat. Stir to fully melt the sugar, and then bring to a simmer. Add the strips, reduce the heat to low, and cook for 5 minutes. Remove from the heat, cover, and let cool to room temperature.

Line a baking sheet with parchment paper. Fish the zests out of the syrup (save the lemon syrup for another use), and scatter over the prepared baking sheet. Sprinkle with sugar and toss to coat. Set aside, or store in an airtight container at room temperature for up to 3 days.

Truffles Line a 5 x 9-inch loaf pan with parchment paper, letting two sides overhang. (This will make it easier to unmold the truffles later on.)

Place the chocolate in a large mixing bowl. Heat the cream to a simmer, either in a small saucepan on the stovetop or in the microwave. Pour the piping hot cream over the chocolate. Let set for 2 minutes then whisk to combine. If the chocolate doesn't fully melt, microwave for 5 seconds at a time at medium power, whisking after each time to verify whether the chocolate is fully melted. Chocolate burns very easily, so be very careful not to overheat it. Stir in the preserved lemon rind and the lemon zest.

Pour the chocolate mixture into the prepared loaf pan. Use a pastry knife or spatula to smooth out the top. Sprinkle with the Candied Lemon Zest. Refrigerate until firm, at least 2 hours.

Remove the truffles from the pan by pulling on the parchment paper. Use a very sharp knife to cut into neat squares (warming up the blade will help make this easier). Serve, or refrigerate the prepared truffles in an airtight container for up to 1 week.

*See page 115 for photo.

SALTED BUTTER CARAMELS

Makes 72 (¾-inch) square caramels

I've been known to gift homemade salted butter caramels as holiday and hostess gifts. I've been asked for my recipe so many times that it was obvious I needed to include it in this book. Making caramel at home isn't hard, but you do need a candy thermometer to monitor the cooking process. My choice is the basic-but-sturdy Polder thermometer, which you can buy for around $10 online or in specialty shops. Make sure to use the best salted butter you can afford since the flavor of this ingredient is crucial to the final taste of the candy.

¾ cup heavy cream

½ teaspoon vanilla bean paste or 1 teaspoon pure vanilla extract

½ teaspoon fleur de sel, plus more for sprinkling

½ cup maple syrup or corn syrup

1 cup granulated sugar

4 tablespoons salted butter, cubed, room temperature

Line a 9 x 5-inch loaf pan with parchment paper, letting two sides overhang. (This will make it easier to unmold the caramels later on.) Set the pan on a wire rack.

In a small saucepan, combine the cream, vanilla, and fleur de sel. Place over medium heat and bring to a simmer. Turn off the heat and cover to keep warm while you prepare the caramel.

In a medium saucepan, whisk together the syrup and sugar. Add the butter and place over medium-high heat. Whisk until the sugar is fully melted. Clip a candy thermometer

continued

Salted Butter Caramels and Triple Lemon Dark Chocolate Truffles (page 112).

to the side of the pan, making sure the tip of the thermometer is immersed into the caramel mixture. Bring the mixture to a boil and cook, very gently swirling the pan twice to even out the cooking of the caramel, until the temperature reaches 310°F.

Remove the caramel from the heat. Slowly whisk the cream into the caramel. (Be careful as the mixture will release hot steam and bubble up significantly.) Make sure the candy thermometer still dips into the caramel; return to medium heat. Bring to a boil and cook until the temperature reaches 255°F for a soft, chewy caramel. (For a firmer caramel, keep cooking to 260°F.)

Pour the caramel into the prepared pan. Let cool for 10 minutes. Sprinkle with additional fleur de sel and let the caramel cool completely.

Remove the caramel from the pan by pulling on the parchment paper. Use a very sharp knife to cut into neat squares (lightly greasing or warming up the blade will help make this easier). Serve, or refrigerate the caramels in an airtight container for up to 1 week. (Make sure to separate layers with parchment or wax paper to avoid the caramels sticking to each other.) You can also wrap the caramels individually into pieces of wax paper and package them in small bags or boxes to give them as gifts.

DRINKS

À boire

FRUIT AND FLOWER SYRUPS

Makes 1¼ to 1½ cups syrup

Drinks served for *l'apéro* are traditionally lighter on alcohol. The goal is to enjoy a drink but still be able to move on to the rest of your evening afterward. Sparkling, white, and rosé wines are staples, of course, as are kirs and other wine-based drinks, but the popularity of modern, carefully crafted cocktails is quickly rising in France.

When I'm mixing cocktails at home, I like to keep things simple, especially if I'm hosting a crowd. I find that keeping homemade syrups at the back of the fridge is the shortest route to creative cocktail hour drinks; the ones I'm sharing here combine fresh fruits, flowers, and extracts to create fragrant syrups you can transform into a variety of drinks, from virgin spritzers to elaborate cocktails. Make sure to always keep plenty of ice in the freezer, and you'll always be ready for company!

Simple Syrup

You'll need 1 batch of simple syrup for each flavor you want to make.

> ½ cup water
> ½ cup granulated sugar

Blackberry Lavender

> 8–12 blackberries, mashed (about ¼ cup)
> 1 teaspoon dried lavender

Raspberry Rose

12–16 raspberries, mashed (about ¼ cup)

5 dried rose buds

½ teaspoon rose extract (optional)

Lemon Chamomile

Zest strips from 1 lemon

1 tablespoon dried chamomile buds, or 2 tablespoons fresh chamomile buds

Orange Verbena

Zest strips from ½ orange

2 teaspoons verbena tea (about 2 bags), or 2 tablespoons fresh verbena leaves

½ teaspoon orange blossom water (optional)

Strawberry Hibiscus

4-6 strawberries, mashed (about ¼ cup)

1 teaspoon dried hibiscus

To prepare the simple syrup, heat the water and sugar together and stir until the sugar is fully dissolved. Pour the hot syrup into a 2-cup glass jar. Add the ingredients for the flavoring of your choice. Close the jar and gently shake it to combine the ingredients. Let cool to room temperature then refrigerate for 24 hours. Strain and return to the jar. The syrup will keep, refrigerated, for up to 2 weeks.

Spirit and syrup pairing recommendations

- **Blackberry Lavender:** Mezcal, white tequila, gin, or vodka.

- **Lemon Chamomile:** Vodka, white tequila, white rum, gin, or limoncello.

- **Orange Verbena:** Bourbon, Scotch, brandy, rum, cognac, mezcal, absinthe, or vodka.

- **Strawberry Hibiscus:** Rum, mezcal, gin, cognac, or vodka.

- **Raspberry Rose:** Gin, rum, cachaça, vodka, or white port.

EASY COCKTAIL

Makes 1 cocktail

If using fruit juice, pick one to match or complement the fruit used in the syrup you choose.

Ice
1 ounce flavored syrup (page 118)
1 ounce spirit, of choice
1 ounce fresh fruit juice (optional)
Sparkling water

Fill a cocktail shaker and a glass with ice. Add the syrup, spirit, and juice to the shaker. Shake until thoroughly cold. Strain into the glass then top off with sparkling water. Serve immediately.

From left: Sparkling Kir (page 122), Virgin Fizz (page 122), Easy Cocktail, Blackberry Lavender Syrup (page 118).

SPARKLING KIR

Makes 1 cocktail

1 ounce flavored syrup (page 118)
Sparkling white wine

Pour the syrup into a champagne glass. Top off with wine. Serve immediately.

VIRGIN FIZZ

Makes 1 virgin cocktail

Ice
1 ounce flavored syrup (page 118)
Sparkling water
Fresh fruit, for garnish

Fill a glass with ice. Pour in the syrup then top off with sparkling water. Garnish with fruit and serve.

INDEX

123

METRIC CONVERSION CHART

Volume Measurements		Weight Measurements		Temperature Conversion	
U.S.	Metric	U.S.	Metric	Fahrenheit	Celsius
1 teaspoon	5 ml	1/2 ounce	15 g	250	120
1 tablespoon	15 ml	1 ounce	30 g	300	150
1/4 cup	60 ml	3 ounces	90 g	325	160
1/3 cup	75 ml	4 ounces	115 g	350	180
1/2 cup	125 ml	8 ounces	225 g	375	190
2/3 cup	150 ml	12 ounces	350 g	400	200
3/4 cup	175 ml	1 pound	450 g	425	220
1 cup	250 ml	2 1/4 pounds	1 kg	450	230